D0926693

Apple of My Eye

Also by Helene Hanff

84, CHARING CROSS ROAD
THE DUCHESS OF BLOOMSBURY

Helene Hanff   61,731

Apple of My Eye

DOUBLEDAY & COMPANY, INC., GARDEN CITY, NEW YORK
1978

Library of Congress Cataloging in Publication Data

Hanff, Helene.
 Apple of my eye.

 1. New York (City)—Description—Tours. I. Title.
F128.18.H354   917.47'1'044
ISBN: 0-385-12483-x
Library of Congress Catalog Card Number 77–76241

PRINTED IN THE UNITED STATES OF AMERICA
First Edition in the United States of America

When New York City went bankrupt (became poor?), its Department of Civic Affairs and Public Events was closed down; and all the duties formerly shared by several executives devolved upon one small Assistant to the Mayor, still in her thirties, named Arlene Wolff.

Arlene creates mammoth street fairs and city-wide holiday celebrations at almost no cost to the city. She does it by commandeering the services of New York's business community, hotels, airlines and public relations firms, and the Police, Fire, Sanitation and Parks departments, and galvanizing all of them into a work force to brighten the lives of New Yorkers all year round.

She does this in addition to her routine duties of planning and managing all official entertainments and receptions for distinguished visitors given by the Mayor of Gracie Mansion, and arranging all citations and awards given by the city to individuals and organizations.

Her awesome talents in the performance of these duties and her selfless devotion to the City of New York, are equaled only by her talent for selfless and devoted friendship.

This book is for her.

To Arlene from Helene. With love.

Christmas 1976

PHOTO CREDITS

Apple of My Eye

1. NEW YORKERS' IDEA OF A GREAT WAY TO SPEND A HOT JUNE SUNDAY
One of Arlene's street fairs (see dedication).

On April Fool's Day, I came home from a meeting with a publisher, hurried through my apartment-house lobby and told all the tenants waiting at the elevator:

"I've got the dream assignment of all time! I'm going to write copy for a book of photographs of New York City!"

Everybody congratulated me. Riding up in the elevator everybody assured me that a book of photographs with copy by a knowledgeable New Yorker like me would help to counteract the city's unfortunate image.

As soon as I had my coat off, I phoned all my friends and told them the news.

"If I'm an expert on nothing else," I said, "I'm an expert on New York, New York!"

Everybody agreed.

Confining the book to "New York, New York" ("So nice they named it twice," it says on T-shirts all over town this season) meant I wouldn't have to do research on Brooklyn or Queens, both of which are out on Long Island, or on the Bronx, which is up on the New York State mainland, or on Staten Island, which is off the coast of New Jersey. All I was going to have to worry about was the original City of New York on Manhattan Island, where I've lived all my adult life and which, as I told my best friend on the phone, I knew like the back of my hand.

That was on Thursday. On Friday I hurried round to my local branch of the New York Public Library and brought home three books about New York. They were old books; the library can't afford to buy new ones due to the city's financial crisis. But I thought they'd give me the facts and figures I ought to have. I got paper and pencil, carried all three books to the desk, opened all three to page 1 and began dipping into all three at once.

Each book had a list of Must See sights and I began copying out those that had made all three lists:

> The Statue of Liberty
> Wall Street and the Stock Exchange
> Times Square
> Empire State Building
> Rockefeller Center
> United Nations
> The Cloisters
> Grant's Tomb

Grant's Tomb?

I put the pencil down, closed the books and stared at the list. I'd never been to the Statue of Liberty. I'd never been to Wall Street or the Stock

Exchange. I'd been to Times Square, and while it's admittedly a sight these days, it's not the kind you put on anybody's Must See list.

I'd been to the top of the Empire State Building, but the Empire State Building was no longer the world's or the city's tallest building and it no longer had the best view of the New York skyline. It had been superseded by the 110-story World Trade Center, and I'd never been to the World Trade Center.

I'd been in and out of certain Rockefeller Plaza buildings several hundred times, but I'd never taken a tour of the Center. And while I had been to the Cloisters once, years ago, I had only a hazy memory of it.

If I have to add this, I'd never been to Grant's Tomb.

I stewed over the list for a few hours. Then I remembered that Patsy Gibbs was coming to lunch on Monday, and I put the whole problem out of my mind till then. Patsy Gibbs was not only a native New Yorker; she was a Radcliffe graduate married to a Harvard graduate, and their son and daughter were both currently Harvard students. Nobody else I knew combined a native's knowledge of New York with access to two generations of Harvard brains.

Patsy and I had met and become friends back in the early sixties as members of the same neighborhood Democratic club. Then she had moved to the West Side and in recent years we'd seen each other very rarely. I considered it providential that we'd run into each other on Fifth Avenue the week before and had made a lunch date for Monday.

Patsy arrived promptly at one. (She's generally called "Pat," but to me the name "Pat" suggests somebody tall, cool and unruffled. Patsy Gibbs is small, excitable and enthusiastic, with a face that registers emotion like a silent-movie heroine, and I've always called her Patsy.)

"Listen, I need your help," I said as I took her coat. "I'm writing copy for a book of photos of New York and I've just discovered I've never been to any of the tourist attractions! Would you believe I'm going to have to go see the Statue of Liberty?"

I was about to ask her what I ought to know about the statue when the look on her face stopped me. Patsy was staring at me with intense, imploring eagerness.

"Can I come with you?" she pleaded. "I've never been there!"

"You've never been to the Statue of Liberty?" I demanded. "But you were born here!"

"My parents took me when I was five but I don't really remember it," said Patsy. "And when my kids were old enough, they went with their grandparents, so I never got to go!" And again with that beseeching look: "Can I come with you? Would you mind?"

I did not ask her whether she had an equal craving to tour the New York Stock Exchange or stand on the 110th-floor outdoor observation platform of the World Trade Center, and I did not ask how she felt about Grant's Tomb.

"Of course you can come with me, Patsy," I said kindly.

"I keep telling you it's Pat!" she said impatiently. "Patsy doesn't suit me!"

Believe me, it was about to.

Friday, April 9

Pride goeth.

During the rest of that week, I copied information industriously out of the library books. At the end of the week I knew how long the Statue of Liberty's right arm was, how many tons the George Washington Bridge's cables weighed and how many acres of floor space were occupied by the American Museum of Natural History.

I also had a page of earnest "Instructions for Tourists." (1. Stop at the nearest bank or subway station and buy bus-and-subway tokens. 2. Stop at the Convention & Visitors Bureau for sightseeing brochures and maps. Etc.) And I had made a tentative list of sights to see and trips to take. On the night before our scheduled trip to the Statue of Liberty, I was feeling in complete command of the entire project, and was studying the Yellow Pages, when Patsy phoned.

"We have to take different subways down there!" she said in a panicky voice. "We've never been down around Battery Park! How are we going to find each other?"

"We're not going by subway," I said. "I've drawn up a list of Instructions for Tourists, and Item 3 on the list is: 'Don't take subways, take buses.' You can't see New York from a subway window. So I thought we'd take a regular sightseeing bus down to Lower Manhattan, to see what it's like, and then get off the bus at Battery Park and go out to the Statue."

"Oh great!" said Patsy enthusiastically. "I've always wanted to take a sightseeing bus. Where do we get it?"

"Well, I'm looking at the ads in the Yellow Pages—" I said. And Patsy said:

"Wait, I'll get the phone book."

When she came back, I said:

"Page 1671," and we studied the bus company ads.

"The Port Authority has the biggest ad," said Patsy. "You want to take that one?"

"The Port Authority Bus Terminal," I said, "runs from Eighth Avenue to Ninth, they don't have signs to tell you which way is Eighth and which is Ninth, and there are always thousands of people streaming in and out of both entrances and up and down the escalators. You and I are both small, I'm nearsighted, we both panic easily and we'd never find each other."

We settled on a smaller bus company in the west Forties and arranged to meet on the sidewalk in front of the bus office at nine-thirty A.M. for the ten o'clock tour of Lower Manhattan.

We met on time. (I got off the Fifth Avenue bus and ran half a block to the bus office and was just in time to see Patsy running half a block from Sixth Avenue; it turned out we were both fanatically prompt.) We bought our tickets and then went up the block to a drug store, climbed on counter stools and ordered coffee. I took out of my shoulder bag the large composition book I'd bought for note-taking and showed Patsy my collection of Facts-and-Figures.

Patsy looked impressed as she read them.

"This is going to be a very heavy tourist guide," she said a little nervously.

"Well, I want to do it right," I said complacently. At which moment a fat woman in a fur coat sitting on the counter stool next to me turned to us and demanded:

"Where's Cartier's?"

I stared at her blankly. I don't live a Cartier life.

"It's on Fifth Avenue," Patsy told her.

"Yes, I know that, dear," said the fat woman. "Where on Fifth?" No answer. Patsy doesn't live a Cartier life either.

"Have you ever been to Tiffany's?" I said. "It's a beautiful store, it's—"

"Tiffany's is on the southeast corner of Fifty-seventh and Fifth," said Patsy. "It's a very famous—"

"No, dear. Cartier's," said the fat lady firmly. "Never mind, I'll find it."

We walked back to the bus depot in subdued silence. Ten or twelve tourists were boarding the bus and we filed in after them. The bus had a heavy roof, narrow windows and poor visibility. We took seats in the back and the bus moved out of the dingy side street and rolled down a West Side avenue past more dingy West Forties streets. I stared out of the dirty window, very tense.

"Why does he have to drive through the dreariest streets in New York?" I said to Patsy. "Why can't he go down Fifth?"

"This is a two-hour bus trip and you're not allowed to smoke and there's no john," said Patsy morosely. "Write that down, it's the kind of information people need."

The bus rolled down into the garment district and the guide called everybody's attention to the fur trolleys and heavy racks of dresses being pushed along the sidewalk. I went on fuming. The garment district wasn't pretty. Anything that wasn't pretty I didn't want visitors to see.

At Thirty-fourth Street the bus turned east, and as we came to Fifth Avenue the guide announced dramatically:

"Straight ahead, on your right, folks, is the Empire State Building!" And everybody looked out the right-hand windows and saw the restaurant on the ground floor of the Empire State Building. What else can you see out of a narrow window on a solidly roofed bus?

Patsy slid way down in her seat and twisted sideways and peered up through the dirty window.

"Lie down," she advised the other passengers. "If you lie down and look up sideways you can almost see the top."

"They ought to open these windows so people can lean out and look up," I said loudly. "In New York, you have to remember to look Up."

The bus proceeded down the only dull stretch of Fifth Avenue and then turned east again and the guide announced joyfully:

"We're coming to the Bowery, folks! New York's Skid Row! Watch out your windows for the Bowery bums. Sometimes you can see 'em layin' in the gutter sleepin' it off!"

This galvanized the passengers. They half rose out of their seats and pressed their noses to the windows. As the bus moved slowly along the Bowery, a wide avenue lined with missions, some of the passengers ran across the aisle to peer out the opposite windows in the hope of seeing bums in the gutter.

"Bowery bums are a big draw!" Patsy murmured in surprise. As luck would have it, there were only two or three bums out that morning and they were standing up.

The bus made its first stop in Chinatown and we all got out and filed into a Buddhist temple and then into an adjoining curio shop, full of the usual cheap souvenirs-of-New-York and some fine jade jewelry. Then we came out and stood on the sidewalk for a few minutes, looking up and down Pell Street at the huge Chinese signs that hung from upper-story tenement windows and dwarfed the Chinese vegetable markets and restaurants huddled below them. After this we were herded back in the bus, which rolled on down toward Lower Manhattan.

On the way, we passed a huge construction site with a giant sign above it reading CONFUCIUS PLAZA, and Patsy and I were so absorbed in speculating about this that we didn't notice much else along the way. As the bus careened down along the eastern rim of Lower Manhattan to the bottom of the island, Patsy said uncertainly:

"Do you get the feeling we're missing something?"

"I get the feeling we're missing everything," I said. "This is no way to see New York."

At Battery Park the passengers were invited to leave the bus again and walk along the river's edge for a few minutes. As I stepped down from the bus, Patsy, ahead of me, spotted a ticket booth with a sign reading: "Liberty Island Ferry. Statue of Liberty."

"Come on!" she called, and we raced for the ticket booth and bought the last two tickets for a boat which was just about to pull away from shore. Clambering aboard it, we felt as if we'd been let out of school.

We made our way to the far rail of the ferry and hung over the edge, staring out at the statue. Liberty stood with her back to us.

"I should have known that," I said. "She's facing the immigrant ships that sailed in from Europe; she's holding the torch up for them, not for us. She can afford to turn her back on us; we have it made."

"Look back!" said Patsy sharply. And I turned and looked back at the

2. AND, IN THE BACKGROUND
Confucius Plaza. Lower floors complete, upper floors still under construction.

Lower Manhattan skyline. DO NOT DO THIS. You'll have plenty of time to stare at the skyline on your return trip. On your way out to the statue you have to keep your eyes on her; you'll have only one chance, as the ferry rounds Liberty Island, to see her face, the torch in her hand, the Declaration of Independence in the crook of her left arm and the broken shackles at her right foot. And just once, you have to see her, face to face. Not because she's a work of art; for all I know, she isn't. You have to see her face because if you're an American, she's the symbol of what you're supposed to be. Looking at her, I had a sudden memory of Franklin Roosevelt beginning a formal address to a convention of the D.A.R. with:

"My fellow immigrants."

Across the water from Liberty Island we could see the abandoned, ruined buildings of Ellis Island, which the federal government closed down years ago. Looking from those buildings to the statue, I felt a fierce pride that my city was still making room for the "huddled masses" nobody else wanted, even while it went bankrupt caring for them.

The ferry guide told us the boat would be back to pick us up in an hour and a quarter, and Patsy said:

"What are we going to do with that much time?" Neither of us knew, till we saw it, that inside the pedestal of the statue there's a remarkable Immigration Museum.

The exhibits include photographs of the tense, hopeful faces of immigrants peering out at us from under their Old Country shawls, and photographs of the involuntary, hopeless immigrants chained together in the holds of slave ships, staring at us with bewildered eyes.

There's a room containing twelve talking statues, mostly of Revolutionary War heroes, each of whom describes his contribution to his adopted country in English heavily accented by his native France, Poland, Germany, Scotland or Ireland.

23

"She can afford to turn her back on us; we have it made."

Patsy charged up to every statue, listened to its recital and then charged back to me like a gnat:

"Did you hear that? Write that down! Did you hear the ones on this side? Are you writing down what each one did?"

I used to write American history books for children, so I said with annoyance:

"I don't need to write everything down! I know who James Wilson and L'Enfant were!"

"You do?" said Patsy, round-eyed. "I never heard of most of these people!"

So much for Harvard, I thought smugly.

I pointed to the statue of one Tadeusz Kosciuszko and said graciously:

"I will tell you about him, because every New Yorker knows his name. More or less."

"I don't," said Patsy meekly. "How do you pronounce it?"

"Ko*shoo*sko," I said. "He was a Polish engineer, he came over here to fight for the American cause and General Washington put him in charge of building West Point. Now: have you ever listened to a New York City traffic report in the morning? Have you ever heard the New York City Police Department give you the traffic conditions on the Kosky-Osko bridge?"

"Sure," said Patsy.

"Well," I said, "the Kosky-Osko bridge was named for Kosciuszko, the Polish engineer who built West Point. Kosky-Osko is the closest a New York cop can get to Koshoosko."

"How do you know all that?" Patsy marveled. I could have answered honestly: "We had a Polish super in our building who told me how to pronounce it," but I didn't; I just glanced around to see whether any other tourists were impressed by my story—and that's how I discovered we were the only two tourists left in the museum. We bolted out of there and had to run the length of the island at top speed to catch the ferry, which was just about to pull away without us.

"You didn't take the elevator to the top and stand under the statue's face," said Patsy, when we'd caught our breath. "You should have done that for the tourists."

"Why didn't you tell me?" I demanded. "What do I have you along for?"

"I mentioned it." said Patsy. "You didn't hear me and I wasn't going to repeat it. My only childhood memory of the statue is of standing on that outdoor platform, three hundred and five feet above sea level, terrified out of my mind. I'm afraid of heights."

We were hanging over the rail staring at the Lower Manhattan skyline at the time. And since the skyline is dominated by the twin towers of the World Trade Center, I realized I had a problem. I'd read somewhere that the World Trade Center's 110th-floor observation deck is a quarter of a mile above the ground, and sooner or later I was going to have to get Patsy up there. It's an absolute Must for tourists, and I certainly wasn't going up there alone; I'm afraid of heights myself.

The ferry deposited us at the dock alongside Battery Park and we looked around for a restaurant. We didn't see any. Lower Manhattan, just ahead of us across an intersection, was full of restaurants but we didn't know where to find them.

"Where's Sloppy Louie's?" I asked Patsy. "Isn't that around the docks somewhere?"

"I think it's further up," said Patsy vaguely. If we'd had a map, we'd have seen that we were only a few blocks from Fraunces Tavern, which was not only a restaurant but one of the tourist sights on my list. But we didn't have a map. (Why would we have a map? We lived here.) We had lunch at the only place we could find. It was a dirty, dockside cafeteria.

"You'd think there'd be a downtown restaurant mentioned somewhere in that four pounds of information you copied out," said Patsy, as we slurped lukewarm instant coffee out of paper cups.

"There was," I said. "Fraunces Tavern, but I don't know where it is."

"Has that reopened since the Cubans bombed it?" Patsy asked.

"I thought it was Puerto Rican nationalists," I said. "I don't know whether it's open or not, I'll check it out."

After lunch we toured Battery Park, a broad green strip along the bay at the tip of the island and one of the places guaranteed to bring out the historian in me.

"President Washington," I told Patsy—though I knew from experience that the minute you start a sentence with "President Washington," everybody stops listening—"used to stroll here on summer evenings with his wife and the members of his Cabinet and their wives, back in 1789, when New York was the nation's capital."

By this time, Patsy wasn't even within earshot. There are memorial stones in Battery Park, honoring immigrants who died in their adopted country's wars, and Patsy was darting from stone to stone, rapping out:

"Who's on this slab? Did you write him down? Who's on that slab over there? Did you read this one? Write it down. You're not writing anything down!"

"What do I want with every name on every stone?" I demanded.

"Well, I just think you're being very haphazard about this!" said Patsy. "Somewhere in this book you'd better write:

"*'Everything in this book is half-accurate.'*"

27

It was midafternoon when we finally left the park, crossed the broad intersection and walked up into Lower Manhattan to look for a subway to take us home. But except for occasional jury duty—when you take a subway down to your designated courthouse, spend the day indoors and take the subway home—neither of us had ever really been to Lower Manhattan. Now, as tourists, we were seeing it for the first time and it struck us full in the face.

Lower Manhattan, which contained the original City of New York (and before that, the city of New Amsterdam), was once a town of small, upright houses on narrow, curving streets. The houses are long gone but the narrow, curving streets are still there, transformed into toy canyons by the row on row of jutting skyscrapers along them. And on every narrow street and alley, early skyscrapers have been joined by newer and higher ones, so that glass, steel and chrome towers rise above and behind the stone skyscrapers of the fifties, which themselves rise above the brick buildings of the twenties. The result is so dramatic that as we walked, Patsy would clutch my arm every few minutes and say:

"Look up there!"

And I'd look up and see three skyscrapers rising in a single vertical line, each built a generation later than the one below it, all three in wholly unrelated architectural styles, yet the three together somehow forming a single, harmonious composition.

We didn't notice what streets we were wandering along or what ones we passed; we just walked, open-mouthed, gawking upward. We did stop once. We came to a huge, heavy new building and stopped to stare at it, impressed: because etched in the stone was the name ONE WUI PLAZA.

"The Chinese are really booming!" said Patsy. "One Wui Plaza is finished and Confucius Plaza is going up. Write that down."

I was writing it down when I happened to notice, above the name of the building, the zigzag symbol used to denote electricity.

4. "THE TIP OF THE ISLAND"
*Look left of the ferry boat docking at Battery Park and you'll see the "slabs"
Patsy hopped back and forth among. (And the World Trade Center's twin towers
jutting above the skyline.)*

"Let me ask you something," I said. "Is Western Union an international company?"

(One Wui Plaza did a lot for my morale later on. It kept me from feeling guilty when I didn't write something down every single time Patsy ordered me to.)

We stopped at a Chock Full o' Nuts and climbed on stools and ordered coffee and Patsy ordered a doughnut. We were sipping our coffee peacefully when Patsy said:

"Were we on Wall Street?"

The question filled me with mild hysteria, which I hoped I kept out of my voice.

"Of course we were on Wall Street!" I said. "It was that canyon!"

"They're all canyons," said Patsy absently, chewing her doughnut. She broke off a corner of it and handed it to me. "Taste that."

I tasted it.

"Ambrosia," I said.

"So's their coffee," said Patsy. "Write it down." I looked at her and she said, "I'm serious! All tourists aren't rich. They'll see Chock Full o' Nuts places all over town; they should know you get great coffee and doughnuts there, and good sandwiches, and the service is quick and the places are always clean."

"I'll use it," I said. "I just hope it doesn't go to their head."

We found a subway we could both take as far as Grand Central, and as we went down the steps, Patsy said:

"You'll have to come down here again; we didn't see anything."

"Of course I'm coming down again!" I said, as we put tokens in the turnstile and joined the people on the platform. "I have to do Wall Street, I have to do Fraunces Tavern—and I certainly have to go to the top of the

World Trade Center! That's the one Must in a new tourist book about New York!"

Patsy studied the subway floor.

"I'm afraid of heights," she said.

"So am I," I said.

"No, I mean really afraid," said Patsy. "It's a phobia."

"I'm just as afraid as you are. Don't give yourself airs," I said. Then it occurred to me that she didn't have to go there with me if she didn't want to, and I added hastily: "I probably won't get to it for a while. There are so many other places I have to see."

"Where are you going next?" Patsy asked.

I had no order of preference, and I was so anxious not to press the World Trade Center that I fled clear to the other end of the island.

"The Cloisters," I said.

"Oh, I haven't been up there in years, I used to love that place!" said Patsy.

"I thought I'd go next Thursday," I said casually.

Patsy looked stricken.

"I can't make it Thursday," she said.

The subway screeched into the station and there was no way I could shout, "How about Friday?" without seeming pushy. We squeezed into a subway car and rode to Grand Central without trying to talk. As she left me to change to a West Side subway, Patsy mouthed, "I'll call you." During the rest of the ride home, I looked over my notes and discovered I'd taken no notes at all on Lower Manhattan.

That discovery marked the beginning of a very moody weekend. On Friday night at two in the morning I got out of bed to look up Cartier's in the phone book. (It's at Fifty-second and Fifth.) On Saturday, as I cleaned the apartment, I seesawed between deep gloom and high panic. Instead of being in command of a large project with an admiring Patsy at my side, I saw myself taking solitary trips to places I knew nothing about and—if Lower Manhattan was any criterion—wouldn't know anything about after I'd seen them.

On Sunday I tried to bury myself in the Sunday *Times* as usual. But it's the New York Sunday *Times,* and everything I read pointed an accusing finger at some New York sight I'd forgotten to include in my plans. On Sunday night came the climax. I went to sleep and dreamed I was in the publisher's office. My finished manuscript lay on the desk between us as the publisher, with a sorrowful look, handed me a large, beautifully bound volume, its title in gleaming gold letters reading:

BROOKLYN BOTANIC GARDEN

On Monday morning I got out my 1975 world atlas and, just in case my editor should ask why I hadn't researched all five boroughs, worked out the following reply:

Brooklyn has a larger population than the entire state of Kansas or the state of Oklahoma.

Queens has more people than the twin cities of Minneapolis and St. Paul combined.

The Bronx contains more people than the cities of Cleveland and Boston combined.

Staten Island has almost as large a population as the city of Birmingham.

That leaves New York, New York, the city jazz musicians first dubbed "the Big Apple," situated on a strip of island twelve miles long by less than two miles wide at its widest, which contains more people than live in

Greater Seattle with all its suburbs included, and that's enough territory for one book to cover.

Over lunch I calmed down. I reminded myself that I'd been hired to write copy for photographs which somebody was collecting for me and would eventually send me. The Cloisters was way up at 186th Street, and I had no guarantee the book would include a photograph of it. (I was prejudiced against the Cloisters anyway.) I decided to postpone the trip, and all other sightseeing trips, till the photos came; and after lunch I fled thankfully back to the safe haven of my library books.

At five o'clock, Patsy phoned.

"Hi," she said. "Listen, I changed my dentist date; I can go, Thursday. Where do you want me to meet you?"

Patsy came east, I walked north and we met on the corner of Seventy-
ninth and Madison for coffee before taking a Madison Avenue bus up to
the Cloisters. It was a sunny April morning and we ordered coffee-to-go
and carried our containers over to Fifth, to the Seventy-ninth Street park
entrance. We sat on one of the benches beside the lawn that rolls up to
Dog Hill. We were therefore sitting with our backs to the Metropolitan
Museum of Art, which is the only way I will ever consent to sit.

The Metropolitan Museum of Art is one of the world's great museums.
It is also a sprawling, ugly pile of gray stone, which you won't realize
when you go there because you'll enter through the front doors on Fifth
Avenue, and the museum's Fifth Avenue façade is impressive. It extends
from Eighty-first to Eighty-fifth Street and is New York's answer to Trafal-

gar Square: on any fine day, you'll see fifty or sixty people sunning themselves on the broad front steps. Flanking the steps are fountains, and at night when the façade and the fountains are illuminated, the museum looks seductively beautiful.

The Metropolitan Museum has great European and American collections, great Egyptian collections, Greek and Roman collections, medieval collections and Far and Near East collections. It has a concert hall, a pleasant courtyard cafeteria on the ground floor and a private parking lot. All of this occupies thirty-seven acres, and I don't know how many additional acres the museum will occupy when its two new buildings, one to the north of the main building and one to the south, are completed. What I do know is that all of its acres were torn out of Central Park, which does not belong to the Metropolitan Museum of Art, it belongs to me. Me and a million other New Yorkers for whom life in New York would be unthinkable without it.

Wherefore, when Patsy glanced over her shoulder at the museum, barely visible behind the ugly wall around its huge construction site, and asked, "Have you been in the Lehman Wing?" I said:

"I have not. I spent a solid year watching the museum's bulldozers and derricks trample down old trees and rip huge, gaping holes in one of the park's loveliest stretches to put that wing up. Now I'm watching a newer and bigger demolition starting all over again."

"Do you ever go to concerts in the Grace Rainey Rogers?" Patsy asked me. "It's a perfect size for chamber music. I love that hall. And I love the Islamic collection. And the costume exhibits. I guess I love a lot of it."

"Most people do. So would I, if it had a heart," I said. "Will you tell me why, in this skyscraper city, a three-story museum can't build *Up?* Why does it always have to build on the ground, destroying more and more of Central Park?"

5. METROPOLITAN MUSEUM OF ART
A very great museum popular with millions of people. Unpopular with friends of Central Park, of whom I am one.

"The Cloisters," said Patsy neutrally, "is part of the Metropolitan Museum."

"I know it is," I said. "And I consider it very broad-minded of me to be going on a day's outing just to see it."

We went back to Madison and got on a No. 4 bus and looked out the windows at the shops. Madison Avenue is an incredible street; there's nothing you can't buy on it, from designer clothes to housewares, from pastry to paintings. The most expensive stores are in the Sixties and Seventies, but there are shop windows to look at out of a bus window all the way up through the Nineties.

It wasn't till the bus crawled up through the early Hundreds that I said to Patsy:

"I don't work on weekends—Saturdays I clean and Sundays I lie down—but I should've made an exception for the Cloisters. The Culture Bus would have got us up there much quicker."

"Does it go up as far as the Cloisters?" asked Patsy. "Wait a minute!" And she darted down to the front of the bus and spoke to the driver, and came back with the Culture Bus Loop I folder in her hand. She was right: the Culture Bus doesn't go uptown as far as the Cloisters. But it will take you everywhere else mentioned in this book, and it's the greatest New York invention since the Mets.

There are two Culture Bus routes: Loop I goes uptown and stops at twenty-two tourist sights; Loop II goes downtown and makes twenty-nine stops in Lower Manhattan and Brooklyn. This is how they work:

There's a Culture Bus stop at every few blocks along the major avenues. You get on and buy one ticket which is good for the entire day. When the bus comes to the first sightseeing spot you want to visit, you get off the bus and see the sight at your leisure. Then you go back to the bus stop and another Culture Bus comes along and takes you to the next sight you want to see. A bus comes by every twenty minutes, and your ticket entitles you to get on and off at as many stops as you like.

At 110th Street the bus turned west along the northern boundary of Central Park, and as it turned north up Riverside Drive, Patsy got galvanized and started rapping out sights for me to write down.

"Hundred-and-twelfth Street! If they sit on the right, and look over that way, they can see the spires of the Cathedral of St. John the Divine. . . . Hundred-and-fifteenth! Columbia University. Well, you can't see much of it from here but put it down anyway. . . . Hundred-and-twenty-fifth!

6.   GEORGE WASHINGTON BRIDGE

Riverside Church. No, wait. Tell them to look out the back window till the bus gets to . . . to . . . One-twenty-eighth. If they look out the back window at a Hundred-and-twenty-eighth, they can see the Riverside Church bell tower."

I didn't say anything. The Columbia–Riverside–St. John's–Grant's Tomb area was a separate day's outing and I had no intention of going on that dreary safari by myself.

The bus rolled on up into Washington Heights and Patsy said:

"Hundred-and-seventy-ninth! George Washington Bridge!"

"Listen, I'm supposed to make a big thing out of that bridge, it's a Top Ten Sight," I said. "It's beautiful at night, but what else can you say about the George Washington Bridge?"

"It gets you home from Jersey," said Patsy.

An hour and a half after it had left Seventy-ninth Street, the bus turned in at a parking lot at the foot of the Cloisters. We stepped out and had to crane our necks to look up at the rambling stone structure. The museum is set on a high eminence overlooking the Hudson, and from the bus parking lot it is only reached by several flights of high, steep stone steps. We were halfway up them when Patsy suddenly said:

"I'll be right back," and shot back down the steps and disappeared. I went on climbing and waited for her at the top. Standing there, looking through the entrance to an ancient monastery, it occurred to me that the Cloisters would be preposterous anywhere in the world but in a country as new as my own.

Financed in the 1930s by John D. Rockefeller, Jr., the museum contains a thirteenth-century cloister from an abbey in the South of France, a chapter house from a twelfth-century abbey in Gascony, a reconstructed twelfth-century cloister from the eastern Pyrenees, a thirteenth-century Gothic portal from Burgundy and stonework from a twelfth-century church in southwestern France. All of these sections and fragments of ancient buildings had been pulled down, stone by stone, shipped across the Atlantic, reassembled and reconstructed and set on a high hill in New York, New York. To Europeans watching the dismantling of ruined abbeys and chapter houses, it must have seemed a Mad Scientist project only an American billionaire would finance.

But no European can imagine being born in a country which was a wilderness three hundred years ago, in which a building seven hundred years old is literally unimaginable. John D., Jr., knew that millions of Americans had no hope of seeing Europe, but might manage to see New York. Since his countrymen couldn't travel abroad to see medieval architecture, he brought medieval architecture to them.

Patsy came running back up the fifty or sixty stone steps and when she had caught her breath, said:

"I talked to a guard. People driving up don't have to worry about the steps. There's a ramp for cars that goes up to the Cloisters. Anybody coming by bus who can't climb steps should call in advance, and somebody here will meet them and take them up in an elevator."

We went through the entrance hall and up to a desk where a woman sat behind a pile of folders. Next to the pile of folders was a sign. Patsy and I stared at that sign.

Most New York museums these days are reduced, by inflation and rising costs, to asking a small admission fee or voluntary contribution. The Cloisters, like the Met, is listed in the Convention & Visitors Bureau guide as

requesting a voluntary contribution. "Pay what you wish," says the Visitors Guide. But what the sign on the desk said was:

"Suggested Contribution: $1.75"

Patsy was shocked.

"That's too much!" she said. "Suppose a tourist family comes up here? Say a man drives up with his wife and three kids and maybe the kids' grandmother. He could get all the way up here thinking it's a free museum, and then get cleaned out of ten or twelve bucks! For the smallest museum in town."

I was too angry to answer. I took out two one-dollar bills and laid them down on the desk. The woman behind the desk looked at them, and then coldly at me, and then coldly at Patsy.

"Is this for *both* of you?" she asked.

"It is," I said, stonily refusing to let her intimidate me. But I live here and I hate the Metropolitan Museum with a passion and she couldn't intimidate me. She could intimidate you. DON'T LET HER. If you want to make a contribution, it will help the museum to stay open. But remind yourself that your contribution is *voluntary*. If the woman at the desk forgets that, remind her.

The dark, monastic interiors calmed us down. The chapels are starkly bare, their ancient stone walls, altars and tables unornamented except for a few sculptured figures of saints, and high, narrow stained-glass windows. On a few of the walls were medieval French and Flemish tapestries borrowed from the museum's Tapestry Room. The arched doorways of the chapels led out into the cloister gardens, and the airy grace of the gardens accentuated the austerity within.

There was one exhibit which rather haunted me. Referred to in the official booklet only once, by the unamplified word "reliquaries," there stood on display on the bare floor of one chapel several ancient stone coffins. Each coffin bore on its lid a full-length effigy of the man or woman buried in it. One, for instance, bore the effigy of a young woman identified as:

Marguerite
d. 1277
daughter of Robert
Second Baron of Neuberg
Normandy

She was probably laid to rest in a monastery near her father's estates. And you suddenly think how bizarre it is that seven hundred years later she should have been uprooted and transported thousands of miles to a continent she never knew existed, to be put on public display in a city and civilization she could never have imagined. I'm very grateful to John D. Rockefeller, Jr. But is she?

It was one-thirty when we finally left the main building to look for the cafeteria Patsy remembered was somewhere on the grounds. We asked a guard for directions and he said:

"Just walk down that way about a quarter of a mile. You can't miss it."

And he pointed the way. But he was pointing to two parallel paths. The inner path, next to the Cloisters, was crowded with tourists, so we took the empty, outer path nearer the river. (The inner path was crowded because it led to the cafeteria; but that was the kind of horse-sense conclusion neither of us in all our travels ever managed to reach, let alone jump to.)

People tend to think of this island as being level ground. It is not. In New York, "downtown" and "uptown" are literal words, and if you're a walker you're well advised to remember that "downtown" is downhill and "uptown" is uphill. You won't notice this in midtown Manhattan, where the incline is very gradual. In uptown Manhattan the incline can, without warning, become surrealistic. Patsy and I, being deep in conversation as we walked, didn't notice that our path was running gradually downhill while the adjoining path was running gradually uphill. We were still gravely discussing the significance of the Cloisters and I was making a few more notes, when Patsy said:

"Something's wrong. We've been walking for half an hour and he said it was only a quarter of a mile."

We peered ahead and saw nothing that looked like a cafeteria. Then I happened to glance to our right.

"Where's the other path?" I said.

The inner path had entirely disappeared. We were walking along a single path by the side of a fifteen-foot-high stone cliff. A man came walking toward us on the path and Patsy stopped him.

"Can you tell us where the cafeteria is?" she asked him.

"What cafeteria?" he said.

"They told us there was a cafeteria on the Cloisters grounds," I said.

"Oh, the *Cloisters!*" he said. "The Cloisters is up there"—and he pointed up at the top of the cliff.

"How do we get there?" Patsy asked him.

"You're walking away from it," he said. "The Cloisters is back that way." And he pointed us back the way we'd come. We turned around and went back to Square One and started over, along the inner path, and by the time we finally reached the cafeteria we'd had a healthy two-mile hike.

We revived over sandwiches and coffee, at an outdoor table in the sun, and then set off on a tour of Fort Tryon Park.

"This must have been an old fort," I said. "It's named for William Tryon; he was one of the British governors of New York."

Fort Tryon Park is a pleasant green rectangle overlooking the Hudson, with recessed stone benches along stone paths. Today, the benches were all occupied by elderly women reading or knitting in the sun. Most of them probably remember the park long before the Cloisters arrived in it. The land surrounding the fort was owned by the Rockefellers, who gave it to the city for use as a park at the time of World War I. By the early thirties it included a promenade, a playground and a pool. Then in 1938 came the Cloisters, and took up most of it, and the park is now very much smaller. (See Metropolitan Museum.)

Across the Hudson from us were the opulent new apartment houses perched along the cliffs of the Jersey Palisades, built not to attract Jerseyites but to attract New Yorkers.

"People in this town are crazy," I said. "Thousands of them work in New York all day long, and then trek all the way up the Hudson and across the river to New Jersey, just to look at New York at night."

"Well, the views are spectacular," said Patsy.

"I know, but isn't that going a little far for a view?" I said. "You don't have to move to another state to get a good view of New York City!"

For a second, Patsy didn't answer. She was looking tense.

"All right," she said finally. "If you're determined to go to the top of the Trade Center we'd better go there next, before I lose my nerve."

"Tuesday?" I said. "It's supposed to be less crowded early in the week."

"All right," she said, and as we headed back to the parking lot, she added, "I warn you I'm not going to like it."

"Neither am I!" I said.

Throughout its construction, the World Trade Center was cordially detested by all New Yorkers. The unpopular Rockefeller brothers were so closely involved in the financing that for a while the twin towers were known as Nelson and David; and the giant buildings are owned by the even more unpopular Port Authority, which was not created to build and own huge office towers. Plus which, the financially desperate city didn't need two new 110-story office buildings and couldn't afford to supply them with services. And to cap it off, the rumor among the fifty thousand office drones who worked in the buildings was that the elevators shook, especially up around the eighty-fifth floor (a rumor I did not think it necessary to pass on to Patsy).

The bus followed the same route back and Patsy said:

"Make a note: they can take a subway home from the Cloisters."

"They have to take one subway ride anyway," I said, "just for people-watching." (The variety of human sizes, shapes, colors and faces you'll see on one New York subway car is a living, breathing world atlas.) "Listen, should we make a list of one-way avenues—Fifth-Avenue-buses-go-down, Madison-buses-go-up and so forth—so visitors won't stand on an Up avenue waiting for a Down bus?"

"If they're standing on Fifth Avenue they'll see the traffic's all going one way," said Patsy. Then she said, "What are you going to do if you have to mention Sixth? What are you going to call it?"

"I'm going to call it Sixth Avenue," I said. "Did you ever hear anybody call it anything else?"

"Then you'll have to explain it," said Patsy.

"Okay, I'll explain it," I said.

The late, great Mayor of New York Fiorello H. La Guardia once remarked:

"When I make a mistake, it's a beaut."

Well, Hizzoner's most enduring beaut was committed against Sixth Avenue. Back in the forties, Fiorello got carried away one year by Pan-American Day—or maybe it was Week—and announced that in honor of Pan-America, Sixth Avenue was henceforth to be known as The Avenue of the Americas. Nobody thought he meant the change to be permanent, but he did.

46

All the Sixth Avenue street signs came down and new signs went up reading "AVE. OF AMERICAS." Every place of business on the avenue had to change the address on its stationery and in the phone book. A couple of decades later, when new skyscraper office towers went up along midtown Sixth Avenue, every corporation in every building naturally had to list its address as "Avenue of the Americas."

But somehow the name didn't take. To the people who lived here, Sixth Avenue flatly declined to be known as the Avenue of the Americas. It went right on being Sixth Avenue. Thirty years later it's still Sixth Avenue, and it's obviously never going to be anything else. The chief sufferer from Fiorello's beaut, therefore, is the hapless visitor.

You'll come to New York one day and go shopping in Saks Fifth Avenue, and when you come out of Saks you'll stop a passerby and ask him if he can direct you to Radio City Music Hall. And the passerby will point west and say:

"One block over, on Sixth Avenue."

And you'll walk one block over, and when you get there you'll check the street sign, and the street sign will say "AVE. OF AMERICAS." So you'll stop another passerby and say:

"Pardon me, can you tell me where Sixth Avenue is?"

To which there is no possible answer except:

"You're standing on it."

The night before we were to go down to Lower Manhattan, I called Patsy and gave her the itinerary:

"Wall Street, Trinity Church, the World Trade Center and Fraunces Tavern," I said, slipping the Trade Center in as if it were just one more ground-level attraction.

"How do you want to go down?" Patsy asked. "We've taken one West Side bus. Do you want to take an East Side bus down and see the Lower East Side?"

"I have to do that on foot," I said. "I want to go down to Orchard Street on a Sunday; it's one of those sights I've heard about all my life and never seen."

"Oh, great!" said Patsy. "And we can walk down and see Wall-Street-on-a-Sunday; it's supposed to be a ghost town. Make a note."

48

And I made a note, laying the groundwork for what we would look back on as Blockbuster Sunday.

"What about tomorrow? You want to take a Second Avenue bus anyway?" Patsy asked. "Is there anything for tourists to see on Second?"

"Not much," I said. "It's mostly for people who live on it or near it. You know: supermarkets, neighborhood stores, thrift shops."

"Nothing else?" Harvard probed.

"OTB parlors," I said.

OTB stands for Off-Track Betting. It's a legal way for New Yorkers to bet on the horses, and was devised by the city as a painless way to extract from its citizens the extra dollars it so badly needed. (Then the state discovered OTB was profitable and took it over, and now the state runs it and hogs the money.) OTB parlors are storefronts, and some neighborhood block associations wage battles to keep the gambling parlors from opening in their neighborhoods, and while I don't mind them that much, they don't exactly beautify the landscape.

"Let's save time and take a subway down," I said to Patsy, "and get off at the Wall Street station so we won't miss Wall Street again."

We got off at Wall Street and when we came up the subway steps we found ourselves on the sidewalk in front of Trinity Church. It faced the beginning or end of Wall Street, we weren't sure which.

Trinity was one of the city's fashionable Anglican churches back in pre-Revolutionary days (becoming Episcopal after the war). The building has been twice destroyed and rebuilt since then, and is a simple Gothic church, with a narrow steeple that was once the city's tallest spire and tranquilly refuses to look either shrunken or out of place among the towering skyscrapers. But it wasn't the church, it was the churchyard I'd come to see. Alexander Hamilton is buried there. So is Albert Gallatin, whom I'm much fonder of. (He was Jefferson's Secretary of the Treasury.) So

Trinity Church at the entrance to Wall Street—where banks hang out identifying flags the way London's Lombard Street banks hang out symbols. (You wouldn't think banks had that much imagination.)

when we came out of the church and I tried the churchyard gate and found it locked, I was very disappointed and glad I hadn't told Patsy who was in there. (I keep assuming other people *care* where dead statesmen are buried.)

"Would One Wall Street be at this end or the other?" I asked Patsy.

"I don't know," she said. "What's there?"

"Wall Street got its name from a wall Peter Stuyvesant built to keep out pirates. We all know it never did keep out pirates and it was torn down a couple of centuries ago, but there's a plaque on the building at Number One Wall Street marking the spot where the wall began."

"Let's find it," said Patsy, starting across the street. We found the building on the corner directly opposite Trinity Church. It was a huge bank building, home of the Irving Trust (and I hope Washington Irving had nothing to do with the founding of it). Next to the name was the address: No. One Wall. We hunted along the walls for the plaque and didn't find it. But on the side wall we found a large, pale square in the stone, with four holes at the corners, marking the spot where the plaque had been.

"Somebody stole it," I said.

"Let's go ask," said Patsy, and sprinted around the corner and in through the imposing front doors. I followed her as she stepped up to the first desk she came to, and asked the dignified gentleman behind it if he knew anything about the missing plaque.

"Vandals took it, I'm afraid," he said regretfully.

"How long ago?" asked Patsy.

"Oh, quite some time ago," he said.

"Well, the plaque had no historical value," I said. "It was just a plaque. Couldn't the bank afford to replace it?"

He gave me a gently reproving look.

"I'm sure that's being done," he said.

When we came out, Patsy said:

"Make a note to come back next month and see if the new plaque is up."

"You mean you believe him?" I demanded. "You think a bank is going to run out and have a new plaque made? A *bank*?"

"Make a note," said Patsy implacably. "We'll come back down and see."

I made a note.

One thing about the World Trade Center: you don't need a map to find **it**. With our eyes on the severe twin towers jutting skyward, we steered a zigzag course through winding streets until we came to an intersection seething with traffic, across the street from it. As we waited for a green light, we looked across the street and saw, in front of the Trade Center and blocking the entrance to it, cement mixers, mounds of earth, piles of wooden boards and the rest of the construction mess out of which the Center's landscaped plaza will have emerged by the time you read this.

"You know the problem with this book?" I said to Patsy. "I want to write about the Trade Center Plaza and I can't because it isn't there yet. I want to write about Radio City Music Hall and I'm not sure it'll still be there when the book comes out. No other city on earth has such a mania for tearing down the old to build the new—which I approve of. My theory is that since New Yorkers mostly come here from somewhere else, they have no interest in the city's past; they come with big plans for its future. And on a narrow strip of island, you can't build the future without tear-

52

ing down the past first; there isn't room for both. But it's a headache when you're writing a book about it."

We crossed the intersection and picked our way through the mess to the unfinished door of World Trade Center Two, where the observation deck is. We walked into the lobby and I said:

"Welcome to the twenty-first century."

(And what's startling about that, is that in the next two weeks I was to read the same words in two descriptions of the Center lobby.)

The lobby is mostly white marble and seven stories high. Far up on the walls are Gothic oval windows, bizarrely churchlike; and the height and depth, and the whiteness and the church windows, create the effect of a science-fiction interior.

Two or three stories above the lobby floor is a mezzanine deck which encircles the lobby; you take an escalator up there to buy tickets to the 107th-floor observatory, from which an escalator takes you on up to the tallest outdoor observation platform in the world, on the 110th floor.

It was a cloudy day and the sign over the ticket booth warned: "Visibility: 5 miles." There were very few people on line and I said to Patsy:

"Should we wait and come back on a clear day?"

"We're here," said Patsy grimly. "We're going through with it."

Fifteen or twenty of us were herded into an elevator, and the door slid shut. The elevator shot up to the 107th floor in a matter of seconds—and they're right, it shakes; and your ears pop. At the 107th floor the door opened and relief flooded us: The vast floor was enclosed by an unobstructed expanse of heavy windows that ran clear round the deck. Hand in hand, bravely, we approached the windows.

There's a bench inside each window. Between the bench and the window is a heavy brass railing you can hang onto as you look down (and you'll hang onto it). Stenciled in each window is a small map of the street

9. TWIN TRADE CENTER TOWERS
*rising a quarter of a mile above the ground—and you're going up to the top,
no matter how your stomach feels about it.*

below it, with the sights and buildings labeled. You grasp the railing and look straight down a quarter of a mile, into Wall Street or Battery Park or whatever is below your particular window. And then you look up and out, at eye level, at all five boroughs and all six great bridges but mostly at the city itself. From this bottommost tip of the island the whole of New York is spread out before you, its thousand skyscrapers fused into a single, improbable vision of "topless towers." For us, they shone against the gray sky as if the sun were on them.

Seen from those windows, the New York skyline was more an entity than Wren's London or L'Enfant's Washington. No one could look at it without asking: "Who built it?" If you consult the library books, you'll be told that the Empire State Building was designed by Shreve, Land & Harmon, and that Rockefeller Center was created by Corbet, Harrison & MacMurray, Hood & Foulhoux, Reinhard & Hofmeister. Yes, but who? What senior member of the firm drafting plans for the Lever Building said, "Suppose we used green grass . . ."? Who of the Seagram architects first said tentatively: "What about bronze? . . ." Whose pencil drew the spectacular sweeping curve of 9 West Fifty-seventh Street? Who built it? Anon., that's who. Nobody built the New York skyline. Nobody by the thousands.

We stared out with no sense of height, just awe.

"That's some dying city," I said.

And suddenly, irrationally, I gloried in the highhanded, high-flying, damn-your-eyes audacity that had sent the Trade Center's twin columns

rising impudently above the skyline at the moment when New York was declared to be dying, and so deep in debt it couldn't afford workers to dispose of the Center's trash, police its plaza or put out its fires.

We moved from window seat to window seat, silently gawking, except when Patsy, sitting before a window map that included Fraunces Tavern, announced that she had studied the location and knew exactly how to find it so that afternoon would present no problems.

There are telescopes by the windows and several tourists were glued to them, probably hunting the block in Queens they lived on. (Locating Uncle Harry's house in Connecticut would have to wait for a clearer day.)

Next to the elevators was the steep escalator which led up to the 110th-floor observation deck. Patsy circled it warily and said:

"Lets wait and get on behind other people."

We stepped on behind a broad-backed man and his broad-backed wife. Patsy was so ashen with terror that I forgot my own in my obligation to reassure her.

"Did you know," I said conversationally, "that in 1770 New York City went bankrupt? Governor Colden had to write to London for permission to float a loan."

"Keep talking," said Patsy.

"The Crown," I said, "vetoed the loan."

"Oh, right," said Patsy.

"Well, what with all the taxes New York was paying to London, the town got very worked up," I went on. "And the Crown grudgingly reconsidered and said, 'All right, you can have a loan. But just this once. After this, if you're still in trouble, you can drop dead.' Well, right after that, the Revolutionary War broke out and the Crown lost all its colonies."

We stepped off the escalator onto an outdoor platform sensibly designed to prevent suicides and provide a needed anticlimax to the observ-

56

atory three floors below. The platform we stood on reminded both of us of a resort boardwalk. It's a broad wood and cement floor, the railing hidden behind thick shrubbery. A few feet below it is another broad boardwalk extending further out on all sides, so that when you look down, the lower boardwalk is all you can see. Then you look out, and the splendor of the city smites you all over again with "astonishment of the heart," as it says in the Bible.

It was one-thirty when we finally took the elevator back down to the lobby to look for a restaurant open to the public. A new restaurant had just opened on the 107th floor of Tower One, but we knew we wouldn't be admitted to it. (That restaurant—Windows on the World—is now New York's most celebrated restaurant. But it was an added source of irritation at first, because it opened as a private club from which the general public was excluded at lunchtime. This caused such public fury that the restaurant backed down later, and today, non-club members are admitted to lunch on payment of a steep cover charge in addition to the cost of the lunch. At night, dinner at the restaurant is like a ticket to a Broadway hit musical: you have to reserve your place months in advance. If you're not rich, go there for Sunday brunch, when there's no cover charge; or, better still, stop at the cocktail lounge after dusk—it's open from four to seven—and see the diamond-studded night city.)

We found an attractive coffee shop in one of the two lobbies, I forget which. It had small tables along cushioned banquettes. We found an empty table and a waitress brought us menus. After studying mine, I was happily watching attractive lunch platters go by on trays when I realized that Patsy, her menu unopened, was staring at me.

"What's the matter?" I asked.

"You're writing this book for tourists," she said. "We can*not* eat lunch in the basement of the world's tallest building."

"It's not the basement, it's the ground floor," I said.

"It's the basement," said Patsy. "We are sitting in the basement of the tallest building in the world."

"The 110-story Sears Building in Chicago is taller," I said.

Patsy went on staring at me like a stony conscience.

"In Toronto," I said, "there's a Needle that's taller than the Sears Building in Chicago."

Nothing. Patsy's accusing eyes never left my face. So I sighed and gave in and put my shoes back on, and we left the coffee shop and went past a maze of lobby shops and on into the other lobby and up to the information desk, and then around to a bank of elevators which would take us up to the forty-fourth-floor "Sky Lobby," where, we were told, there was a restaurant.

There is definitely a restaurant on the forty-fourth floor. I'm told it's very pleasant and you will probably find it without difficulty. We couldn't find it. We went down a long hall which turned more corners than I thought there were. We went past rabbit-warren office doors and past two of the Center's seven banks of elevators. Finally, when an office worker came along, Patsy stopped her.

"Do you know where we eat up here?" she asked. And the office worker said:

"One flight down, through that door."

We pushed open the door and walked downstairs; and that's how we happened to have lunch in the dirtiest, dreariest office-workers' cafeteria that ever closed for the day just as we were ready for our second cup of coffee.

And, of course, when we got out on the street, Patsy, not having the stenciled window map with her, didn't have any idea where Fraunces Tavern was. However, on our walk from Trinity Church to the Trade

Center we had noticed the wall maps which are a charming feature of the Lower Manhattan landscape. On lampposts and on the walls of buildings, at three- or four-block intervals, is a small map of the immediate area with all the chief points of interest marked, and a bright, black arrow pointing to one spot on the map, with the legend "YOU ARE HERE." We found one such map near the Trade Center and Patsy studied it.

"This map," she said finally, "is upside down. I think we go that way."

We went that way, through small streets we hadn't been on before, and I began to wish somebody we knew would come along. There are two groups of professionals who work in Lower Manhattan: (1) the stockbrokers, bankers, underwriters and accountants who work in the financial district, and (2) the city officials, judges, law clerks and attorneys who work in the City Hall and Courts district. We knew a sprinkling of people in the second group, but of course none of them came by. Finally we stopped a man hurrying by with a briefcase.

"Can you tell us where Fraunces Tavern is?" Patsy asked him.

"I'll be glad to," he said. And he put down his briefcase, took his wallet out of a breast pocket and extracted from the wallet a small map. As he studied it, I was comforted to realize that Lower Manhattan was just enough like London for even the regulars to carry maps, so Patsy and I weren't as dimwitted as we felt.

"Here we are," he said finally, and pointed us down toward Battery Park and then east of it.

We walked down till we came to the broad intersection where, from the Battery Park side, we had first seen Lower Manhattan. But the approach from the upper side was dramatically different. With the skyscrapers behind us, we looked across the intersection to a row of eighteenth-century houses, on a street that was like a little island standing by itself, a forgotten relic of the past. Fraunces stood on the corner nearest us. Being both a historical museum and a popular restaurant, its red brick and white molding looked freshly painted, and its windows, brightly clean, were flossy with white curtains. By contrast, the four houses alongside it looked decayed and abandoned and there was something touching about them, empty and neglected but still stubbornly standing where they had always stood. Then we noticed the last house in the row. Dingier and more dilapidated than its neighbors, it had a sign of life in its bleary ground-floor window. The sign read:

"OTB."

And Patsy was waving at it wildly and I was laughing and crowing "I love this town!" and we almost got run over crossing to Fraunces.

All traces of the bomb damage were gone, and the tavern seemed intact. It's an attractive restaurant, "restored" and self-consciously charming like the Dickens pubs in London. (Though passed off as a restoration, it is in fact a totally new building, constructed in 1907; and its resemblance to the original, beyond a general "period" style, is almost totally conjectural. The only thing authentic about it is the site. Too bad.) We went upstairs to the celebrated room from which General Washington is supposed to have said farewell to his officers. According to an eyewitness, Washington "filled his glass and lifted it and said: 'With a heart full of love and gratitude I now take leave of you.'"

"The officers who were present at the leave-taking," I told Patsy, "very probably included Kosky-Osko."

The museum contains military dispatches, and a few letters and artifacts from the Revolutionary War, as well as the history of Samuel Fraunces, the West Indian who owned the tavern before, during and after the Revolution.

("Race prejudice is a remarkable thing," I said to Patsy. "When the British invaded New York and the patriots fled, the British confiscated all

60

10. FRAUNCES TAVERN ON THE CORNER
and far up the block. . . .

patriot property. When the British marched out and the patriots returned, they confiscated all Tory property. But neither side ever confiscated Sam Fraunces' tavern: he was black, so he didn't count as Tory or patriot. You get the feeling nobody ever thought to ask him which he was.")

It was ten minutes to five when we left Fraunces, so we were just in time for the five o'clock subway rush hour. Maybe, just once, you ought to take a New York subway during the five o'clock rush, to see how the other side of insanity lives. Every subway car is wall-to-wall people. I was pushed nearly to the middle of the car by the crowd entering behind me; and though I had nothing to hang onto, and the train lurched round every bend, the solid wall of bodies kept me upright. I finally managed to work my right arm through enough coats and elbows to get three fingers around the center pole and I counted eleven unrelated hands or parts of hands above and below mine on the pole. Then the train stopped at Grand Central and two thousand more people pushed into the car and I lost my hold entirely. It's not an experience I am up to twice in one week, so when Patsy phoned on Wednesday and said, "I've got tomorrow free. Where to next?" I said:

"Midtown Manhattan. We're entitled to a nice easy one. We're going to spend the day with millionaires."

"Would you believe," I said to Patsy when I met her the next morning, "that there are forty-five museums listed in the Manhattan telephone book?" I consulted my notes and added:

"In addition to the Irish, Chinese, Jewish, Hispanic, American Indian, Black, Primitive and Folk, there are museums of Firefighting, Numismatics, Sports, Jazz and Oceanography. And that's not counting any of the art museums, not even the most famous ones—the Met, the Guggenheim, the Whitney and Moma." (The Museum of Modern Art is on Fifty-third Street, and when you pass it you'll see an enormous navy blue banner floating in the breeze with the acronym MOMA on it.)

"How many do we have to go to?" Patsy asked dubiously.

"I picked out four," I said. "Three have a common denominator: even

tourists who are bored by museums have to see them. They can ignore the museum when they get there. It isn't the museum I want them to see."

"Oh," said Patsy. "Like this one."

We were standing in front of a mansion on Thirty-sixth Street between Park and Madison. Its official name is the Pierpont Morgan Library. It's a two-story mansion built by J. P. Morgan to house his private library and his priceless collection of art objects. And let's say you have no interest in J.P.'s rare porcelains, illuminated medieval manuscripts, Gutenberg Bibles or early children's books, and that since you're not a scholar or collector, you won't be admitted to the reference library. Go anyway. Go there to meet J. Pierpont Morgan.

The mansion was designed as "a Renaissance palazzo built of fitted marble blocks in the classical Greek manner," it says in the brochure. Inside, however, the house abandons the Renaissance and classical Greece in favor of Queen Victoria and Edward VII. You enter a dark, airless hall with heavy mahogany doors opening into two exhibit rooms. After you've seen whatever interests you—the medieval manuscripts in glass cases or the portable Flemish altar on the mantel—climb the dark, heavy mahogany stairs to the second floor, to the East and West Rooms. Do the East Room first. This was J.P.'s private library.

The long gallery above the room is lined with rare and magnificently bound books (which you can't go up the gallery stairs to look at, because you're not a scholar). You'll find a few more books in glass cases and more rare art objects on display. Then go into the West Room, which was Morgan's private study and has been preserved just as he left it. In the West Room, you are in the palpable presence of the owner of the house.

The room is suffocating with mahogany and red plush: heavy dark mahogany tables and chairs, red plush sofa and drapes, and red silk wallpaper. The carved ceiling was imported from a Florentine cathedral. The stained-glass windows were imported from a German cathedral. I don't remember where the massive fireplace was imported from. Dominating the room, extending from the ceiling down to the mantel above the fireplace, is a huge, standing portrait of J. P. Morgan, wearing a red dressing gown that matches the red silk wallpaper. Beneath the enormous canvas, several small items on the mantel pale into insignificance, including a priceless miniature portrait of Martin Luther. Straight-backed mahogany armchairs are set at a respectful distance from the imposing desk they face.

"From behind that desk," the guard on duty informed us proudly, "Mr. Morgan made all the major financial decisions for the Allies in World War I." Kings and queens and heads of state, he told us, came to this room, hat in hand, to negotiate loans with the great J.P.

The room gave me the cold horrors. But history, as somebody once remarked, is not a rummage sale. If you come to New York looking for the history of the United States, the pretty candy box of Fraunces Tavern is not chiefly where you find it.

It was a relief to get out of that oppressive mausoleum into the sunny April morning again.

"Did you know that J. P. Morgan was born in Hartford, Connecticut?" I asked Patsy.

"If that's the beginning of one of your long-winded stories, I don't want to hear it," said Patsy. "Let's start walking toward the Frick even if we don't make it." The Frick Collection was nearly forty blocks away, up at Seventieth and Fifth. "We can stop for coffee on the way."

"Of course we're stopping for coffee on the way," I said. "We're going to Paley Park. I told you we're spending the day with millionaires, I didn't say they were all dead."

Paley Park is on Fifty-third Street between Madison and Fifth, but it's not the open green space the word "park" implies and you have to look sharp or you'll pass it by. It's a narrow hole-in-the-wall park, sandwiched in between two dark buildings, an oasis where you can get coffee and a sandwich to eat at one of its picnic tables, or just sit on a park bench and enjoy the greenery and the waterfall which is the back wall. I read somewhere that William Paley (whose CBS building is only a couple of blocks away on Sixth Avenue) built it for the city's midtown office workers. Those who brought their lunch from home needed a pleasant place to eat it; those who didn't needed to buy sandwiches and coffee at a place less dreary than the cafeterias they could afford. As we got our coffee and took it to a table, I told Patsy:

"William Paley was born in Philadelphia, like me."

She wasn't listening. She was fishing two newspaper clippings out of her handbag. She pushed them across the table to me and said:

"I thought you might have missed these."

Both were from the *Times*. I hadn't missed them, I'd ignored them. One was about the house down in the Twenties somewhere where Teddy Roosevelt was born. The other was about the Morris-Jumel mansion up at 160th Street and St. Nicholas Avenue. Looking at those clippings, I realized that Patsy's Harvard background could be something of a problem.

"With all there is to see in New York," I said, "do you really think tourists are going to want to run down to the Twenties to see Teddy

Roosevelt's birthplace? FDR had a town house on East Sixty-fourth Street and I wasn't even going to bother with that."

"Herbert Hoover," said Patsy thoughtfully, "had a suite at the Waldorf Towers. Well, all right, I guess you can skip presidents' houses. But the Jumel mansion is a Landmark, it was Washington's headquarters during the Revolution."

"I know," I said. "He was there just long enough to lose the Battle of Harlem Heights and abandon New York City," and I changed the subject. I thought I'd disposed of the Jumel mansion and, when we rose to go, I left the clipping on the table. But Patsy, with one of her stony glares, picked it up and stuffed it into my shoulder bag and I knew I hadn't heard the last of it.

The Frick Collection was the finest private art collection in the country when Henry Clay Frick died and left it—and the mansion that houses it— to the people of New York City. (He was born in Pittsburgh.) It's another "palazzo" but entirely white—white stone outside, white stone and marble inside. And as often as we'd both been there, entering it today was almost a shock, coming to it as we did from the somber darkness of the Morgan. The Frick house is all light and air.

You enter a foyer where an oblong white stone pool of very clear green water is flanked by white garden benches and potted trees. You go on into a central hall, the white marble floor as spacious as the gallery rooms opening off it. At the far end of the hall, there's a great marble staircase with the pipes of an organ on the landing. (The keyboard is in a niche by the foot of the staircase.)

I read in S. N. Behrman's *Duveen,* that Frick used to hire an organist to come and play to him on Saturday afternoons. Frick sat in his long gallery, reading *The Saturday Evening Post,* while the organist played "Silver Threads Among the Gold." Never mind: today, you can hear lovely chamber music concerts at the Frick on Sundays at four.

We entered the gallery rooms, where white walls leave all the color to the paintings—and even if (like me) you know nothing about painting, the blaze of colors on the Frick walls will dazzle you.

"Harry Truman," I said, "once said that the Carnegie libraries were steeped in the blood of the Homestead steelworkers."

"Did you see the Goya over the mantelpiece?" said Patsy. "It's incredible."

"The steelworkers at the Homestead plant had gone on strike for a union contract. So of course the plant hired scab labor," I said.

"Look at the little Memling," Patsy murmured. "The light takes your breath away."

"The manager of the Homestead plant brought in three hundred armed Pinkerton guards to protect the scabs. He smuggled them in at night by boat. When the Pinkerton guards' guns weren't enough to break the strike, the governor sent in the state militia."

"Where's the Rembrandt self-portrait?" asked Patsy.

"The guards and the militia cut down the steelworkers in cold blood, and that finally broke the strike," I said. "And for years afterwards, the steel companies didn't have to pay union wages; and Carnegie and the Homestead plant manager lived happily ever after."

"Why do you have to tell me a story like that when I'm trying to see the most fabulous collection in town?" Patsy demanded.

"Because that's how this fabulous place got built," I said. "The manager of the Homestead plant was Henry Clay Frick."

We left the Frick and when I said:

"Next stop: the Cooper-Hewitt Museum of Interior Design," Patsy gave me a sour look.

"I love the Cooper-Hewitt," she said. "I love the Meissen china and the antique wallpaper and the antique textiles—and after your terrible story, I won't be able to enjoy it!"

The Cooper-Hewitt Museum is at Ninety-first and Fifth, in the Carnegie mansion.

As we walked up Fifth Avenue, passing all my favorite East Side streets at intersections on the way, I said:

"How can I get visitors to turn off Madison or Fifth and walk East and explore the side streets in the Sixties and Seventies? When my friend, Nora Doel, came here from London she was bowled over by them. She said the only pictures she'd ever seen of New York were of skyscrapers; she couldn't believe the rows of beautiful houses along the East Side streets."

"I gather," said Patsy politely, "you're not planning to include the West Side in your book."

"I'm doing the West Side next, as a matter of fact," I said virtuously. "I'm going to do Rockefeller Center."

Patsy stopped in her tracks.

"Do you mean to stand there and tell me you call Rockefeller Center the West Side?" she demanded. "Your idea of the West Side being the west side of Fifth Avenue?"

"Rockefeller Center runs west of Fifth almost to Seventh," I said. "And

14. MILLIONAIRE #4
Andrew Carnegie's Fifth Avenue mansion.

you didn't let me finish. We're going to do Rockefeller Center and Lincoln Center, and I'll mention the theater district. I'm not chasing all the way over to Duffy Square just to look at it, but I'll mention that Duffy Square is at Forty-seventh and Broadway, and there's a booth there called TKTS where you can get half-price theater tickets for any show on Broadway that isn't sold out for that day's performance. And unless you really insist on dragging me through the Natural History Museum to stare at reconstructed dinosaurs, I don't know what else there is to see on the West Side."

"If you can lower yourself to come to my house," said Patsy, "I'll show you."

We turned into the side entrance of the Carnegie mansion, to be met by a locked gate and a huge sign telling us the museum was closed for the summer "for renovation" and would reopen as a branch of the Smithsonian Institution. By the time you read this, it will have become a much larger and more impressive museum of interior design, with displays of medieval and Byzantine textiles and collections of drawings, ancient and modern. And maybe the remodeled Carnegie mansion will have an interior less grim and forbidding than it used to be.

"Okay, now where?" asked Patsy as we turned away from the locked gate. "Gracie Mansion?"

Gracie Mansion, in the Eighties next to the East River, is not a museum; it's the official residence of the Mayor of New York. Technically, it's a tourist attraction but it's surrounded by a wall.

"What can a tourist see of Gracie Mansion but the wall and the driveway?" I said. "Do you want to know the only way an ordinary citizen can get a really good view of Gracie Mansion? Have a baby. A couple expecting a baby should reserve a room at Doctors Hospital and ask for a room with a river view. As soon as the baby's born, the parents can hang out the

74

window and watch the goings on in the Gracie Mansion garden and living room and dining room and even a couple of bedrooms."

We were walking up Fifth and Patsy said:

"Well, do you mind if I ask where we're going?"

"I thought after all these millionaires," I said, "we'd go visit one pauper." And we went on up to 104th Street and Fifth, to the Museum of the City of New-York. It's a small, manageable museum in a brown brick house with white stone trim, recording the city's history from the Dutch days onward in four floors of engaging artifacts. (The top, fifth floor contains rooms from the old Vanderbilt mansion but is closed to the public these days because the city can't afford guards to keep it open.)

Everybody's favorite exhibit is the collection of antique toys and dolls together with a group of marvelously detailed dolls' houses, complete down to handmade linens in the hope chests. Patsy, being a rabid theater-goer, had to be dragged away from the Broadway theater exhibit. (It changes every few months and may deal with an era or just a single personality in the theater, and is always complete with three-sheet posters, programs, costumes, photographs and recorded songs.)

There are period rooms from every quarter-century, and until you see the life-size mannequins in each room, you don't know how tall mankind has grown in three hundred years.

There's one more exhibit which I love and which ruined my day. It's a group of dioramas depicting the history of the New York Stock Exchange, from the famous first meeting of merchants under a buttonwood tree to the nineteenth-century day when ticker tape replaced runners, and including a spectacular three-dimensional view of Wall Street during the Blizzard of '88. And it was as we were peering into this one that the hideous oversight struck me. I must have turned a sickly color because Patsy asked:

15. PAUPER
Museum of the City of New York.

"What's the matter?"

"I made sure we saw Wall Street because it's on every book's Must See list," I said. "And I forgot that the reason *why* it's on every Must See list is it's the home of the world-famous New York Stock Exchange. Which we didn't even look for, much less take a tour of."

"Oh, right," said Patsy. I looked at her and she looked pleased. "I guess we'll have to go back down there," she said.

"To tell you the truth," I said, "I was going back down anyway. Alexander Hamilton and Albert Gallatin are buried in Trinity churchyard and I want to see their graves. The cemetery was locked when we were there but I thought I'd phone Trinity—"

"It wasn't locked," said Patsy. "The side door was open. I wondered why you didn't want to go in."

I had two martinis that night before dinner instead of my usual one-and-a-half. I didn't mind having to go back down to Lower Manhattan again (and wouldn't have minded if I'd known we'd have to go back down there not once more but twice). What I minded was the discovery that I was no more in command of the project than I'd been when we started.

Like most cities, New York is a collection of small neighborhoods. I live in Lenox Hill, surrounded by colleges (Hunter, Marymount Manhattan, Mannes Music), singles (young and old), monster new apartment houses and dogs. Above Lenox Hill is Yorkville, old and formerly German, with a main street—Eighty-sixth Street—that looks like any small-town Main Street except that the bakeries, restaurants and small stores along it are German, Swiss and Hungarian as well as American. Below me is Sutton Place, small and rich and quiet, and below that Beekman Place, even smaller and richer and quieter. Then you come to Murray Hill and then to Tudor City—a compact small town built above the city and reached by high stone steps—and then Madison Square and Gramercy Park, and so forth. Most of these neighborhoods have their local free weekly newspaper, their political clubs, block associations and Community Planning Boards.

Patsy lives on Central Park West, in a section of it which is also a neighborhood: a row of old and famous apartment houses, now co-operatively owned by the families who live in them. Above her neighborhood and slightly west of it is the Riverside Drive neighborhood, thick with Columbia professors' families, and above that is Morningside Heights (see next chapter). Below Patsy's, there's Lincoln Towers—an apartment-house complex behind Lincoln Center which is its own self-contained community—and below that you come to Chelsea and Clinton and the Village, and so forth. They, too, have their throwaway newspapers and political clubs and block associations and Planning Boards.

BUT: all the neighborhoods above and below and including mine are strung together into a psychological unit and share a common attitude and common rules of behavior. And all the neighborhoods above and below and including Patsy's are strung together into a psychological unit and share a common attitude and common rules of behavior. And the two units are poles apart and don't understand each other. Because *unlike* other cities, New York is literally split down the middle, by Fifth Avenue, into East and West Sides. And never the twain shall meet on any common ground but Saving New York City.

Fifth Avenue itself, which runs through the center of town from below Eighth Street to 110th, is neutral territory. But the street signs at intersections along the Avenue mark off the separate Sides for you. Say you're standing in front of St. Patrick's Cathedral and you see a sign on the downtown corner reading "E 50 St." Cross the avenue and you'll see a sign on the corner reading "W 50 St."

And just so you'll know what Side you're on at any given moment, if you're on Fifth and you walk east, you'll come to Madison, Park, Lexing-

ton, Third, Second and First, in that order. If you're on Fifth and you walk west, you'll come to Sixth, Seventh, Broadway, Eighth, Ninth and Tenth. That's in midtown. When you go up to Fifty-ninth, where the park begins, you'll see that Central Park itself separates East from West, being bounded on the East by Fifth Avenue and on the West by Central Park West (an extension of Eighth Avenue), where Patsy lives. Both Fifth Avenue and Central Park West have fine views of the park, which is very evenhanded. Today the East Side is basically richer than the West; fifty years ago it was the other way around, which is also evenhanded.

What the West Side has always had that the East Side has never had is a concentration of the city's great performing-arts centers: the Broadway theaters, Carnegie Hall, Lincoln Center, the giant television network centers in skyscrapers along Sixth Avenue, and Rockefeller Center, which begins at Fifth Avenue and mushrooms west.

That's the background. The underlying differences between East and West Siders can wait till we get over to Patsy's.

Patsy and I met that morning at 30 Rockefeller Plaza ("30 Rock" to the people who work there) and went up to the tour desk in the lobby and discovered there are two separate tours: Tour I, a guided tour of Rockefeller Center, and Tour II, a backstage tour of NBC's radio and television studios. Tour I tickets were available. Tour II was on strike.

"Should we do the Center tour now and come back for the NBC tour when the strike is over?" I suggested.

"—and we'll get home tonight and hear on the six o'clock news that the strike's just been settled," said Patsy. "Let's wait a week."

So we left Rockefeller Center and walked up to Fifty-seventh and then turned west, toward Lincoln Center, which starts at Sixty-fourth Street. We turned west on Fifty-seventh partly because it's a beautiful street to walk along: it has fine shops and art galleries and Carnegie Hall. But there was another reason—and I promise this is the last time I'll bore you with street directions, but this one is something nobody ever warns visitors about, and it always gets them into trouble.

If you're standing in front of 1 East Fifty-fourth Street and you're looking for 1 West Fifty-fourth Street, you'll find it right across Fifth Avenue or, as they say, right-across-the-street. But if you're standing in front of 1 East *Sixty*-fourth Street and you're looking for 1 West Sixty-fourth Street, it's not across the street, it's clear across Central Park, and you ask somebody where you get a "crosstown" bus to take you over to the West Side. Patsy and I avoided this by turning west before we got to Fifty-ninth, where the park begins.

"We get the tour tickets at Avery Fisher Hall," I said, as we came within the sight of the Lincoln Center buildings.

"Philharmonic Hall," Patsy corrected grimly.

We got our tickets at Philharmonic/Avery Fisher Hall for the tour which took us through four of the main buildings—(1) a two-level theater for stage plays known as the Vivian Beaumont Theater upstairs and the Mitzi Newhouse Theater downstairs; (2) the New York State Theater (home of the New York City Ballet and the New York City Opera companies); (3) Avery Fisher/Philharmonic; and (4) the Metropolitan Opera House. (The best Lincoln Center tour is the backstage tour of the Met, which you can only take during the opera season, October to March, and which includes rehearsals.) The tour didn't include the Juilliard School of Music and its adjoining concert hall, alias Alice Tully Hall.

"The trouble with this tour," said Patsy as we hung over the rail of one of the Met's promenade decks, "is that it's in the daytime, and these buildings have to be seen at night. You have to be part of the audience. You have to see the chandeliers lit, and the promenade decks during intermission—when you look down at all the marvelous people in the lobby, all looking the way you'd like to look."

"I'll tell you a story about this place," I said. "My friend Arlene ran a political fund-raising party here a few years ago. There's a lobby on the Met mezzanine big enough for a cocktail party for two hundred people and that's where she had it. I was volunteer ticket-taker—the party was for a candidate our club was backing—and my ticket table was at the top of the grand staircase. The party was on a rainy winter Thursday, at five, and people came direct from their offices without going home to dress. You know how they look—the lawyers and law clerks and local officials and club workers who go to that kind of party. I sat at my table at the top of the staircase and watched them push through the Met doors in bunches, in a hurry to be out of the rain, all of them looking wet and frazzled and out of sorts. When they started up the sweeping marble staircase they all hunched forward, the way people do when they're climbing steps.

"But when they reached the third or fourth step, they began to change. Coming up that staircase, they straightened, almost imperceptibly at first. They became erect, they began to climb more slowly—and about halfway up, every man almost unconsciously took the arm of the woman next to him. By the time they reached the top, the men were stepping aside to let the women pass, and the women were sweeping regally up to my table and smiling at me and saying, 'Good afternoon,' which they don't normally say to a ticket-taker. It was extraordinary."

Outside the Vivian Beaumont Theater, on a wall beyond the long reflecting pool, there's a plaque honoring John D. Rockefeller III, identi-

fied as "the prime mover" behind the creation of Lincoln Center back in the early sixties. On the plaque is a statement by Rockefeller which begins: "The arts are not for the privileged few but for the many."

"That's what's special about New York," I said. "The concern for 'the many' that people have when they come here, or acquire after they get here. That's why a handful of rich men and women have done so much for the city."

"Like Frick," said Patsy.

"Like Frick and Carnegie," I agreed. "This overcrowded city is where they chose to live; and it's the hordes of people of all kinds, 'the many,' that they left their great collections to and built concert halls for. In view of which, we shouldn't resent the new names on all these buildings."

"It's still Philharmonic Hall to me," said Patsy flatly.

"Personally," I said, "I wish Avery Fisher had declined to have Philharmonic Hall renamed in his honor, no matter how much money he spent to have the acoustics corrected. And I wish Alice Tully had said, 'No, no, just call it Juilliard Concert Hall!' But let's face it: you and I both know that while art may be for 'the many,' it always has to be financed by the few. And fair's fair: readers of a book about New York have a right to know what Avery Fisher and Vivian Beaumont and Mitzi Newhouse and Alice Tully have in common."

After lunch, we walked up Central Park West to Patsy's apartment house, passing side streets lined with large Victorian brownstones and graystones as we went.

Back in the early years of the century, the West Side was a middle- and upper-income residential area. (The East Side in those days was most famous for its slums, where railroad laborers lived and died in Old Law and New Law tenements. Old Law tenements had air shafts; New Law tenements had to have windows.) Those were the days when the West Side was the opulent New York of Lillian Russell and Diamond Jim Brady, of majestic hotels and fine town houses. Today, many of the hotels are ancient and decayed, and house welfare families. The rows of Victorian houses have long since become moldering rooming houses, but more and more young families have begun buying them, ready to spend years remodeling and rewiring to convert them into modern one-family homes. The old houses have high ceilings, fireplaces, long halls and spacious rooms all reminiscent of an earlier age, which, to West Siders, is the secret of their charm.

"A friend of mine lived over here for ten years," I told Patsy. "She had a floor-through in an old brownstone. Then I met her in my supermarket one day and she told me she'd moved into a new building up the block from me. She said, 'I got up one morning and thought: Enough of this Old Charm, I want a modern kitchen.'"

Patsy nodded.

"We lived on the East Side for six years," she said, "before I suddenly knew I didn't care if the molding peeled, I wanted to live where I could feel roots and a sense of the past around me."

By this time we were approaching the American Museum of Natural History, which runs from Seventy-seventh to Eighty-first Street and has a sixty-seven-foot long, sixteen-foot high, thirty-ton reconstructed brontosaurus in Brontosaurus Hall, if that interests you. Also stuffed elephants, stuffed lions and stuffed rhinoceroses.

"Do we have to do the monster?" I asked.

"They have a fabulous jewel collection," said Patsy. Then she said, "No, forget it, you could spend a month in there and not see everything, and not find your way out again."

"I'll tell you what," I said. "We'll skip Natural History and go see the Hayden Planetarium Sky Show. There's a show at three, I made a note of it. We can just make it."

Patsy threw me a noncommittal look.

"Our class went there when I was eight," she said. "My kids both had to go with their classes when they were eight."

"Well, I've never been," I said—and we went.

We were ushered into the Sky Theater, where the ceiling was a simulated sky full of stars, and we took seats among the twenty or thirty school children waiting for the show to begin. A lecturer came out on stage and welcomed us. Then the theater darkened, the overhead sky-ceiling brightened and the show began.

"Twinkle, twinkle, little star, How I wonder what you are!" said the lecturer, and then proceeded to explain what a star was, in terms nobody without an M.S. in Astronomy could understand.

The children squirmed and whispered and looked up at the star-studded ceiling with relief whenever the patterns changed. At the end of an hour, the lecturer recited triumphantly:

"Twinkle, twinkle, little quasar, Now I know what YOU are!" and the house lights came up and we got out of there.

"You could have warned me!" I said. And Patsy said:

"Well, you go every fifteen years thinking maybe it's gotten better."

We adjourned to her house for coffee. And you need only walk into her foyer to know why families live on the West Side.

My own apartment is listed by the landlord as a "2½-room studio" and is actually a large living room with a small alcove. The living room counts as one room, the alcove is a second room because it has a window, and the kitchen is half a room because it doesn't have a window. The bathroom they throw in free. Real estate arithmetic. And the statement I am about to make is not an exaggeration and not meant to be humor; it's a flat fact:

You could put my entire apartment in Patsy Gibbs' foyer. In the *foyer*. Opening off the foyer are more rooms and bigger rooms than you'll find in a modern ranch house. There's a large living room, an equally large library, a dining room that seats twelve easily (eighteen if it has to), three bedrooms, three baths, a large bedroom for the housekeeper (remodeled from two small rooms) and a double kitchen (which includes a former butler's pantry), where eight people can sit down to breakfast.

"Anne Jackson and Eli Wallach have an apartment the size of yours, if you'll pardon my name-dropping," I said, as Patsy made coffee. "I got lost in theirs once. I could hear Annie calling me and I went from room to room and couldn't find her; she had to come and get me."

"When we first moved in, we had a baby-sitter coming one night," said Patsy, "and we waited and waited for her, and finally I called her house and her mother said she'd left forty minutes before. So we went looking for her. She'd been sitting in the library for half an hour."

Though living space is mainly what families move to the West Side for, you find singles and childless couples over there, too; and living space and charm are not what chiefly attract them. The real difference between the East Side and West Side is in the people. They not only think and behave differently from each other; they look different.

Generally speaking, West Siders look dowdy, scholarly and slightly down-at-heel, and the look has nothing to do with money. They look like what a great many of them are: scholars, intellectuals, dedicated professionals, all of whom regard shopping for clothes as a colossal waste of time. East Siders, on the other hand, look chic. Appearances are important to them. From which you'll correctly deduce that East Siders are conventional and proper, part of the Establishment and in awe of it—which God knows, and God be thanked, West Siders are not.

I'll give you an example. Suppose tomorrow's New York *Times* prints the news that JFK airport is building new runways for supersonic jets. The West Side Democratic clubs will charter buses, ride out to JFK and march around the airport with placards reading "NO SST FOR NYC" and "SAVE THE ENVIRONMENT FOR OUR CHILDREN." They'll sing fight songs, have a couple of clashes with the police and turn up on the eleven o'clock TV evening news.

The East Side clubs will hold a dignified debate and then send a telegram to the governor telling him they're against air pollution.

But since families need living space and may move to the West Side to get it, and since singles want modern kitchens and may move to the East Side to get them, both Sides have a certain number of fish-out-of-water. Which explains why Patsy and her husband never joined a West Side club when they moved over there and why I periodically drift away from mine. I love the East Side streets and buildings; but my Establishment neighbors occasionally drive me up the wall and I read wistfully about West Side demonstrations because, psychologically, I belong over there. And Patsy, who loves the West Side for its space and charm, has never set foot in a noisy West Side Democratic club because, psychologically, she belongs over here. (Though Patsy is special: she was born on the West Side, so it's not a Side to her, it's her old Kentucky home.)

Still, the Side you live on influences your thinking and behavior if you live there long enough. I've accepted the Establishment name of Avery Fisher Hall. Patsy will call it Philharmonic Hall for the rest of time.

18. *Gramercy Park (East 20th to 21st Street).*

19. *West 76th Street.*

20. *Bank Street in Greenwich Village (West).*

We had coffee in the living room, before picture windows looking out over Central Park with a breathtaking view of the Central Park South skyline beyond. Then I said:

"It's after five, I have to get home."

"We have one more stop to make," said Patsy.

"Where?" I asked.

"Zabar's," said Patsy.

I'd heard about Zabar's from all my gourmet friends but I'd never been there, so I said:

"I'll go there with you some time. Not today. I'm tired."

Patsy's face registered instant outrage.

"Zabar's is one of the most famous Sights on the West Side!" she said. "Do you realize people like Frank Sinatra have pastrami and bagels flown to them in Europe so they won't starve? You are going to put Zabar's in your book!"

"I'll tell you what I'll do," I said. "I have to tour Morningside Heights—Columbia, Riverside, Grant's Tomb, all that—which is another West Side tour. If you go with me, we'll take a Broadway bus back down and stop off at Zabar's on the way home."

"All right," said Patsy, "but this time you're not going to weasel out of it."

And just like that, I had her committed to the only wearing uptown junket left on my list.

I'll say this for our tour of Morningside Heights: every sight we saw bore the unmistakable stamp: Made in the U.S.A.

We got off the Broadway bus at 112th Street, at the (Episcopal) Cathedral Church of St. John the Divine, which is "the largest Gothic cathedral in the world," according to the church booklet. It is a permanently unfinished cathedral.

The cornerstone was laid in 1892, and for three decades the work went steadily forward, until the completion of the great bell tower in 1930. Then came the Depression, followed by the war decade and war shortages, and in the fifties the great middle-class exodus to the suburbs. By the sixties, the neighborhood had changed from rich to poor, and today there are no plans to finish St. John's. As a clergyman we met there said simply:

"You don't spend millions on a cathedral when people around you are hungry."

The magnificent church seats ten thousand, but since it's a bishop's seat and has no parish, the nave is roped off for great occasions and the average Sunday congregation of three hundred worships in a vestibule chapel inside the front doors.

Patsy and I went down the side aisles to look at the rare tapestries hanging from the scaffolding which was standing along one church wall. Then I moved down to look at the stone pulpit, and Patsy went out onto the altar floor to look at the three fine chairs, two white ones flanking the bishop's red one, all three set against the right-hand altar wall. Suddenly she turned and beckoned me violently, her face purple. I went up and joined her, and Patsy pointed to the wall behind the three chairs. Halfway up the wall hung a telephone. Next to the phone was an intercom board. On the intercom board was a list:

1. Console
2. Power Amp. Room
3. Panel Room
4. Dean
5. Precentor
6. Pulpit
7. Organ
8. Bishop's Throne
9. Recording

"Operator, gimme the Bishop's throne."

There may be an equally efficient intercom system operating off the wall of the high altar at Chartres or Westminster Abbey but somehow you doubt it; it just reeks of American know-how.

We left St. John's and started walking toward 115th Street and Broadway and the entrance to the original quadrangle which contained Columbia College and now contains a fraction of Columbia University's un-

94

dergraduate buildings. Since Morningside Heights is also the home of the Union Theological and Jewish Theological seminaries, it's very much a town-and-gown community; and what startled Patsy and me, in view of all the horrific crime stories we'd read about the area, is that a town-and-gown community is exactly what it looked like.

We were walking in a spacious neighborhood of tree-lined avenues, the solid, substantial fronts of old brick houses hiding the poverty and desperation of both the black and Puerto Rican newcomers and the elderly white holdovers who live there. The lovely green stretch of Riverside Park along the Hudson concealed the fact that the park is considered one of the city's most crime-ridden. Maybe crime only comes out at night there. All I can tell you is that Patsy and I wandered all over the area all day long, and saw only students, professors and clergymen hurrying by, a class of small boys filing into a church school, black and white children playing at the foot of Grant's Tomb and elderly men and women sitting on park benches.

Entering the Columbia quadrangle was like stepping into the set of a 1940s college movie. The ivy-covered buildings and flagstone walks, the students lying on manicured lawns with their noses in textbooks (it was final-exam season) seemed unreal.

We were walking along a stone path, with college buildings on both sides of us, when Patsy announced:

"I have to find a ladies' room."

We stopped a passing student, who pointed to an administration building and said:

"Right over there."

We went into the building and wandered without seeing a washroom. Patsy stopped another student, who sent us through a courtyard and into an annex where we were directed up a flight of steps to an elevator and told to get off at the seventh floor. We went down the seventh-floor hall and around a corner and there at last was a washroom. When we came out, we saw an elevator next to the washroom and we rode down to the ground floor and went out into the quadrangle, unaware that, while we had entered the building through the front door, we'd left it by the back door, and that, furthermore, it wasn't the same building.

You remember those parallel paths at the Cloisters? Well, the Columbia quadrangle also has parallel paths. But since the paths are on opposite sides of college buildings, you only see the one you're walking on. Patsy and I went on our way along a flagstone path, looking at the buildings; and if the path was taking us gradually uphill, we didn't notice it. We just strolled on, admiring the academic scenery, until, with great suddenness, we saw the end of the quadrangle looming ahead and apparently suspended in space. We found ourselves on an open parapet above a fifteen- or twenty-foot drop to a stone courtyard below. If you're afraid of heights, this is not a good place to find yourself. Looking around, I discovered that we were entirely alone. There wasn't a student in sight and the only building nearby presented its windowless back to us. Next to the building I noticed the top of a flight of steps leading down from the outside of the parapet and, without looking at Patsy, I made myself walk over to it and look down.

"It's okay," I called to her. "It's a short flight of steps going down to a landing and there's a building down there."

We ran down the steps, our eyes glued to the landing so they wouldn't stray off to the side and see the twenty-foot gorge.

On the landing we found a large glass door and, peering in, we saw that it was the back door to a gym. The gym was empty. The door was locked. We turned to go back up the steps and saw, for the first time, that they were open, ship's-ladder steps. Patsy went white.

"I can't go up there," she said.

Since the only alternative was to throw ourselves off the parapet, I heard myself say:

"I'll go first."

Sheer guilt drove me up those steps: it was my book we were up there researching (if that's the word for what we were doing). I started up the steps, Patsy close behind so she could keep her eyes on my back. I could hear my breathing. Patsy had stopped breathing altogether; she held her breath till we got safely back up onto solid stone ground. By this time I was too far gone for fear and, throwing off caution, I walked close to the end of the parapet—and saw a long, steep but solid flight of stone steps leading down to the courtyard.

Columbia University has new science buildings and playing fields down on the courtyard level, and there was new construction going on which we ought to have investigated, but by that time we'd lost our taste for Columbia.

What Columbia does not have, as far as we could discover, is a place where nonstudents can eat. Anything. We wandered up and down Broadway and up and down the side streets and finally Patsy stopped a girl going by with books under her arm, and asked if she could tell us "where there's a place to eat around here." The girl recommended Mom Somebody-or-Other's Delicatessen.

"It's the best deli in town," she said earnestly, and pointed us a few blocks further down Broadway.

"Do you want to try it?" Patsy asked when the girl had gone on her way.

"I just want to sit down," I said. Since most delis don't have tables, I thought this meant "No," but Patsy decided it meant "Yes," and she started back down Broadway toward the deli. I followed her, repeating every now and then, "I just want to sit down."

In every neighborhood there's one deli which the local residents believe is the best in town. Since all of Morningside Heights, including the entire populations of Columbia, Union Theological and Jewish Theological, believed Mom Whatsername's to be the best deli in town, there was a long line of customers waiting for service. The line was jammed in between grocery shelves on one side and glass cases of cold meats and salad on the other. Everybody on line was waiting to step up to the glass cases and give one of the two countermen a lunch order for sandwiches and coffee. To go. There weren't any tables.

Patsy streaked back to the end of the line, I followed her fuming, and as the line inched forward, she turned to me now and then to say brightly:

"The line's moving very fast, considering."

After twenty minutes of Considering, we finally got our sandwiches, cole slaw, one milk and two coffees and then carried the bags two blocks to a Riverside Park bench. I was carrying the bag with the cole slaw in it, and the cole slaw dripped all the way over.

We sat on a bench and I chewed my turkey-on-rye-with-Russian in simmering silence until Patsy turned to me, hesitated, and then asked tentatively:

"Do you want me to keep on with this? This sightseeing?" My bad humor dissolved in shock.

"What kind of a question is that?" I demanded. "Here I'm in the middle of giving birth to this important book, and the midwife asks if I want her to keep on with what she's doing!"

"Well, I just realized this morning it's May," said Patsy. "We go away in June when the kids come home from college. I thought I'd better ask how much time you want me to save this month."

"All of it!" I bleated. "We haven't seen anything yet! We have all the major tours to do!"

After lunch we stopped at Riverside Church—known colloquially as "the Rockefeller church" because John D. Rockefeller, Jr., supplied the funds for it. Riverside is another beautiful Gothic church, less ornate and imposing than St. John's. It's probably no more beautiful than the big midtown churches—St. Patrick's, St. Thomas's and St. Bartholomew's—but then, it isn't the building that makes Riverside Church the pride of New York.

As its brochure proclaims, Riverside is "an interracial, interdenominational and international" church. Along with the standard church groups, its three thousand parishioners include a Black Christian Caucus and a Chinese Christian Fellowship. From the days of Harry Emerson Fosdick, its most celebrated preacher, to the present, Riverside has involved itself in every battle for human rights from antiwar protests to migrant-labor legislation to prison reform. And since Martin Luther King, Jr., graced its pulpit as guest preacher in the sixties, we weren't surprised to find that its current roster of ministers includes a woman.

"And I'll bet you," I said to Patsy, "that men who've never had any trouble with the word 'charwoman' or 'cleaning woman' will find it absolutely impossible to say 'clergywoman.'"

Catty-corner from Riverside Church is the tourist attraction which dominates the landscape of Morningside Heights. Grant's Tomb, with its immense granite dome, sat on its hill above the Hudson looking impressive, beautiful and deserted, and we trudged staunchly across the street to it. We went up the broad marble steps and in through the imposing doors, to pay our respects to Ulysses Samuel Grant, the great Union general who won the Civil War, whose military memoirs have been compared with Caesar's, and who as President of the United States a century ago presided over the most corrupt and scandal-ridden administration in the country's hundred-year political history.

21. RIVERSIDE CHURCH
"Interracial, interdenominational, international."

22. GRANT'S TOMB
"Well, at least there are two of them in here instead of just one."

You enter a vast, empty white marble hall, feeling dwarfed by the huge dome above you. You walk to the center of the floor to the rim of a great marble basin. You peer over the rim of the basin down to a floor below, and see two bronze coffins containing the mortal remains of U. S. Grant and his wife, Julia Dent Grant. This is the sight you've come to see, and almost all there is to see.

"It looks like Les Invalides," said Patsy. "Napoleon's tomb."

"I don't know whether that makes it more preposterous or less," I said.

"Well, at least there are two of them in here," said Patsy, looking on the bright side.

Beyond the great hall were two small rooms and we went back to investigate them. On the walls were framed newspaper clippings recounting the history of Grant's life and career, and framed newspaper photographs of the family. And it's nobody's fault that the bearded general and his wife were angular and rawboned, and stared woodenly into the newfangled camera with expressionless faces, but today they look like characters in an Ozark cartoon.

There was one photograph in particular, in which Grant and his wife and children were all sitting bolt upright on the porch of a bolt-upright frame house, which, if it wasn't falling down, could at least have used a paint job. Underneath the photograph was a typewritten caption:

President Grant and his family
on the porch of the Summer
White House at Long Branch, New Jersey.

Patsy and I had to support each other out of there.

A solitary guard was on duty at the door, and when we came out, Patsy asked if there were many visitors to the Tomb.

"Oh, yes," he said. "Every year there's a big ceremony on General Grant's birthday."

"How many people come to it?" Patsy asked.

"Well, the Union Army vets always turned out big for it," he said. "We'd have three–four hundred vets come every year."

"How many came this year?" asked Patsy.

"Well, they've all died off now," he said.

We waited, but he didn't add anything. We thanked him and went down the broad steps and left the deserted shrine and walked over to the Broadway bus stop. And the photographs had been funny and the Tomb outlandish, but old lines were running in my head:

> *The tumult and the shouting dies.*
> *The captains and the kings depart. . . .*
> *Lord God of Hosts, be with us yet,*
> *Lest we forget—lest we forget!*

Going from Grant's Tomb to Zabar's was going from the sublime to the ridiculous or from the ridiculous to the sublime, I'll never be sure which. And if Grant's Tomb was Made in the U.S.A., Zabar's was Made in New York City. Definitely no question.

I don't think anybody's ever counted the number of delicatessens in New York, but there are four within less than two blocks of my apartment house and that's not an unusual number. Every neighborhood has a string of delis and almost all of them make excellent sandwiches, sell good rye bread and pickles and the usual cole slaw, pickled beets, potato, chicken and tuna salad. But Patsy was right: none of them can be remotely compared with Zabar's.

You go in through the front doorway and duck under ten or twelve

103

different kinds of salami hanging on hooks from the ceiling. Way in the back, there's a cheese department it would take two jars of air freshener to neutralize. Between front and back, on the walls and on tables well away from the exotic food cases, there is every item of expensive gourmet kitchen equipment on the market, at considerably less than the market price.

None of which begins to convey the essence of Zabar's. Patsy went looking for the manager and conferred with him, and then came back to me, her arms full of outsized Zabar brochures. When I got home I culled from the brochures the following very incomplete summary of what you can buy at Zabar's, the pride of the West Side, at Eightieth and Broadway:

Fourteen kinds of salami, eight kinds of paté, nine kinds of cooked fish, twelve kinds of salad, seven kings of Hungarian sausages, thirty kinds of bread.

Also smoked beef jerky, fresh caviar, sturgeon, stuffed vine leaves, Hungarian peasant bacon, Polish and Yugoslav mushrooms, Romanian pastrami, and cheese "from every country in Europe."

Not forgetting eleven kinds of tea from every country that grows it, and coffee from Jamaica, Hawaii, Kenya, Tanzania, Guatemala and Mexico.

There's one more attraction to Zabar's. It is New York's only genuine *haute monde* delicatessen. A Zabar's shopping bag is a recognized status symbol. It tells the world you're a cultivated and discriminating gourmet, instead of just another New York shlemiel buying a hot pastrami on rye and a sour pickle to go.

Thursday, May 6

This was our only rainy day. And the rain cut short a tour we weren't all that crazy about, and sent us indoors on a tour we had both taken countless times and which somehow never palls.

Now that Patsy had committed herself, I dispensed with diplomatic overtures and phoned her and said bluntly:

"Thursday we're doing the Village."

"Yich-ch," said Patsy.

Greenwich Village is more than a neighborhood, it's a way of life. People who live there would be miserable living anywhere else. People who don't live there see the Village as a kind of continuous theatrical performance interesting to visit for an evening.

Since the Village is on the West Side (the brief life of a pot-smoking neighborhood called the East Village having begun and ended with the sixties), I said to Patsy:

"I'm taking a Fifth Avenue bus down, just to check out any avenue sights I need to mention. Do you want to go down by subway and meet me?"

"Where?" said Patsy. "Not in the Village?!"

"Meet me on the steps of the church at Twelfth and Fifth and we'll do lower Fifth and the Square first," I said.

"Oh, great, I love it down there," said Patsy and we hung up.

It was sunny enough when I left home and walked to Fifth to catch the bus. One day while you're here, you ought to get on a Fifth Avenue bus up around the Carnegie mansion and ride all the way down to where the avenue ends below Eighth Street; it's the best sightseeing bus I know of. You'll ride down along Central Park with all the museums and old mansions on your left until you come to the Plaza Hotel at Fifty-ninth Street, which marks the beginning of the midtown shopping district—and from there on, you have to try looking out the windows on both sides of the bus at once.

Most of the famous shops are in the Fifties: Bergdorf-Goodman, Tiffany, Bonwit-Teller, I. Miller, Gucci, Cartier, Mark Cross, Saks. (Lord & Taylor is down at Thirty-seventh Street, B. Altman is at Thirty-fourth, and if you walk one block west of Altman's you come to R. H. Macy and Gimbel Bros., she-added-so-as-not-to-slight-anybody.) Spread through the Fifties and Forties you'll see the Avenue's five mammoth bookstores: two Doubleday, one Scribner, Brentano and the very beautiful Rizzoli.

23. THE MACY'S THANKSGIVING DAY PARADE

The newest avenue sight at the moment is the glittering Olympic Tower, midtown Fifth Avenue's first apartment house. Olympic Tower, as Patsy succinctly put it, "has apartments nobody can afford to live in, over stores nobody can afford to buy in."

At Fifty-third on the uptown corner on your right you'll see St. Thomas's Episcopal Church, once New York's most fashionable church, now better known for its wonderful Wednesday noon choral concerts. Don't miss them on any account if you're in town at Christmas or Easter time. Don't worry about how you're dressed. You'll see students pile into the church in blue jeans with their arms full of books, and women with their shopping bags flapping. The rector, John Andrew, is genuinely pleased to see the church jammed and gratified that you like his men's and boys' choirs, and he couldn't care less how you look.

Down below Thirty-fourth I saw one place I'd forgotten. It's just off Fifth, at 1 East Twenty-ninth Street. This one's also an Episcopal church with the official name of the Church of the Transfiguration. And the story has been told a hundred times but I feel like telling it again.

Back in 1871, when theater people were beyond the pale of respectable society, a celebrated actor named Joseph Jefferson wanted to provide a funeral service for a fellow actor who had died penniless. Jefferson went to a fashionable Fifth Avenue church to consult the minister about arrangements.

"I'm afraid we couldn't possibly hold funeral services at our church for that sort of person," said the minister, "but there's a little church around the corner that might help you."

24. THE LITTLE CHURCH AROUND THE CORNER
is also the home of a theater company called the Joseph Jefferson Players.

So Joe Jefferson went to the Little Church Around the Corner, and the church gave his friend Christian burial and has been marrying and burying actors and other disreputable folk ever since. If you stop in during the day and find a wedding in progress, you're welcome to assist at it. After six P.M., the weddings are private.

The church at Twelfth and Fifth, where I was to meet Patsy, and another below it at Tenth and Fifth are both old-fashioned neighborhood churches and typical of lower Fifth, a small, quiet residential neighborhood running from Thirteenth Street down to Eighth, with its side streets extending into the Village.

I got there a little early, which was what I'd hoped to do. When I first came to New York, I used to go down to the New School on West Twelfth Street and the neighborhood is nostalgic for me. The New School—officially the New School for Social Research—is a college for adults. You can earn a B.A. or Ph.D. there and you can take daytime courses; but the New School's early fame stemmed from the fact that it was primarily an evening college for people more interested in an education than a degree. In the forties, its faculty was a haven for scholarly refugees from the universities of Hitler's Europe. Which may, or may not, be what led Senator Joseph McCarthy to label the school "Communist-dominated" in the fifties. This embarrassed the Eisenhower administration somewhat: it turned out John Foster Dulles had once taught at the New School.

I used to go down there two nights a week, for courses in such practical, everyday subjects as Ancient Greek and the Philosophy of Religion. (Our Greek professor was a German and like most Germans he couldn't pronounce *th*. So when pointing to the Greek letters zeta and theta, he'd say, "Zis is a zeta, and *zis* is a *zeta*." And somebody in the class would pipe up: "But professor, you said *that* was a zeta," and he'd say, "Yes, yes, quite right, zat is a *zeta* but *zis* is a *zeta!*") I was wandering along Twelfth

Street remembering all this pleasantly, when Patsy came steaming toward me from Sixth Avenue.

We walked down lower Fifth toward Washington Arch, stopping half a block before the arch to poke into Washington Mews, a cobblestone square lined with former carriage houses once attached to Washington Square mansions. The mews houses are quaint and charming, and looking at them you know you're in, or near, the Village.

"Who owns these?" Patsy asked me.

"N.Y.U.," I said, meaning New York University, which is a private, not a state-owned, university. "The only way you can get to live in a Washington Mews house is to be a big name on the N.Y.U. faculty."

We went on down to Washington Square, created as a park setting for Washington Arch. The arch was built in 1889 to commemorate the centennial of Washington's inauguration—because if Paris had an arch and London had an arch, why shouldn't we have an arch? I-imagine-somebody-said.

We walked along Washington Square North looking at the fine houses of Henry James's day and trying to decide which of them the heiress Catherine Sloper lived in. These houses are also now owned by N.Y.U.

"I was in one of them once," I told Patsy. "They have one horrendous feature. They're all connected by interior doors. By which I mean you can be sitting in your living room in your underwear on a Saturday morning, when a door in your living-room wall slides open and your next-door neighbor walks in from his-or-her living room and says, 'Hi, you busy?' "

We crossed Fifth Avenue to Washington Square West and walked on over to MacDougal Alley—"where the effete meet," said Patsy—which is another mews lined with quaint and charming carriage houses, these privately owned. At MacDougal Alley you are in the Village, and you walk west to reach the heart of it.

With its center of activity around Seventh Avenue, the Village is a maze of short, narrow streets radiating in all directions, some of the streets cutting into each other and then disappearing to reappear a few blocks later way over that way. Patsy had brought a Village map along and she looked up from it to inform me:

"There are two West Fourth Streets, one below Eleventh Street and one above Eleventh Street."

So she put the map away and from then on we just wandered in and out of all the side streets, stumbling by accident on the more famous ones—Bank and Christopher and Morton and Waverly Place—all of them old and quiet with rows of small houses, looking as remote from the sky-scraper city as if they'd been set down in it by mistake.

One of the most attractive streets we saw was St. Luke's Place, the locale of the Audrey Hepburn film *Wait Until Dark,* with neat four-story houses behind wrought-iron railings and high front steps. If you walk along it in the evening, you'll see glimpses of private libraries through the lighted windows of high-ceilinged living rooms. We missed one famous house on West Eleventh Street but as far as I know it's still there, if you want to look for it. A gold plaque identifies it as the "Greta Garbo Home for Wayward Children."

Scattered along the avenues and through the side streets are the Village shops, all of them remorselessly quaint-and-charming. I was taking notes on the items for sale in the shop windows—hand-woven Mexican rugs, Indian sandals, unisex haircuts, Taro cards, astrology charts, handmade ceramics, handmade leather belts and shoes—when Patsy, reading over my shoulder, advised me:

"Just say the whole Village is handmade."

On Bleecker Street there are boutiques named "Elegant Plumage," "Second Childhood" and "Marquis de Suede." Also on Bleecker Street, a

25. ST. LUKE'S PLACE
in "the Village."

Spanish restaurant, an Italian, a Mexican, an Indian and a Moroccan restaurant—and that's on a side street. On Seventh Avenue we passed Greek, Indian, Chinese, Turkish, Japanese and Italian restaurants, all within a span of a few blocks.

HOWEVER: at noon it started to rain, and we thought we'd wait out the shower over an early lunch, and that's how we discovered that most Village restaurants open at five P.M. You have to walk to Sixth Avenue to find a restaurant open for lunch. We found a Greek restaurant open and crowded with N.Y.U. Law School students.

"We made the same mistake with the Village that we made with Lincoln Center," I said to Patsy as we waited for a table. "The Village is another place that has to be seen at night. What tourists ought to do is come down late in the afternoon while it's still light enough to see the houses and shops, and then have dinner and go on to one of the off-off-Broadway coffee-house theaters."

"They don't serve coffee," said Patsy gloomily. (She doesn't drink.)

"Well, whatever they're called," I said.

Off-off-Broadway theaters (which differ from off-Broadway less in professionalism than in the price of the ticket) specialize in new, experimental plays performed in any loft or hole-in-the-wall available. But the ones that are the most fun are those in the back rooms or upstairs rooms of Village restaurants and bars, where the audience sits at small tables and watches the play while sipping sangria or New York State wine. The play may bore you; the audience won't. Which is to say that the real sight-seeing attraction of an evening in the Village is Villagers.

On a warm evening, Seventh Avenue and the streets near it are alive with Villagers, and with the young who live uptown and come down to the Village in the evening. The people—especially the not-so-young—seen on a Village street in the evening look completely unlike all other New

Yorkers. They are colorful, flamboyant, unconventional and uninhibited. The atmosphere is of a friendly, integrated, liberated democracy, or an arty, intellectual Sunset Boulevard, depending on your point of view.

We got a table, and after the waitress took our order for a Greek shish kebab, Patsy fished out of her handbag a folded newspaper article from the Sunday *Times* and handed it to me. It was written by a *Times* architecture critic and was a lecture on How to Look at Buildings.

"I read this one," I said. "I did not think highly of it."

Every time a new building goes up in New York, some critic condemns it in the *Times,* and every time an old building is to be torn down, the Landmarks Preservation Commission issues vehement demands that it be Preserved. Well, the chief New York building the *Times* writer had lectured me on How to Look At was Grand Central Station, which every now and then somebody suggests tearing down, only to be met with screaming objections from the Landmarks Commission.

"Do you know any New Yorker," I asked Patsy, "who personally looks on Grand Central Station with admiration and affection?"

"I hated that place when I was a kid," said Patsy. "We went away to camp from there. Going away you couldn't find the counselors, and coming back you couldn't find your parents."

"Exactly," I said. "You've put your finger on the difference between the experts who want to Preserve old railroad stations and the people who have to use them."

Grand Central Station is a huge, squat stone building sprawling from Forty-second Street to Forty-Fourth and from Lexington past Park to a small avenue, called Vanderbilt, halfway to Madison. It was built early in the century, when architects believed that every building had to have a decoration on top. You see manifestations of this where Patsy lives: fine, tall old apartment houses with fancy cupolas and decorated Cupids on

top. The author of the *Times* article admires that kind of architecture and is particularly fond of the statuary group on top of Grand Central Station, he says it pulls the entire station together. The central figure is supposed to be Mercury—wearing a hat, a loincloth and wings. He's standing by himself on top of the Grand Central clock. Nearby, on both sides of him, reclining pseudo Greeks are looking up at him. All of them sitting around on the roof of a mammoth railroad terminal, pulling it together.

"Do you remember the furor when the old Penn Station was torn down?" I said. "That station was a gloomy horror of a building to come into at night, heavy and dark—and the lights so high overhead they threw deep, gaunt shadows on the stone floor. The Landmarks Preservers had a fit when it came down and a new, clean, light, easy-to-find-your-way-around-in station went up. What was it to them if the old station was a nightmare to people who used it? They didn't use it, they just rode around it in their cars staring learnedly at the architecture and advising us peasants to Preserve it."

So now we're Preserving Grand Central Station. You'd better go look at it while you're here. God knows it's a sight.

We dawdled over lunch, hoping the rain would stop, but it didn't. We phoned Rockefeller Center and the NBC tour was still on strike.

"What other indoor tours do you have on your list?" Patsy asked.

"Only the U.N. and that's one tour I don't need to take," I said. "I know that place by heart. I love it."

"So do I," said Patsy. "I take out-of-towners there first." She sipped her coffee and added, "I wonder how the new hotel is coming."

"What hotel?" I said. "Are they building a hotel over there?"

The U.N. hotel opened before this book went to press; it's the center building with the broken line. Below it, the General Assembly; alongside it, the Secretariat.

So we went out to the street and hailed a cab and told the driver to take us to the United Nations.

"A cab and a restaurant in one day?" Patsy said with an eyebrow raised. "We're ruining our record."

That was the only cab we ever took. But as we settled in the back seat, I said to Patsy:

"I'm tired of cafeteria lunches. From now on, we're going to eat restaurant lunches like respectable tourists." And the cab driver must have heard this because he called back to us:

"You girls wanta see Bowery bums? You wanta see lesbians? I can show you everything! Where're you girls from?"

We told him we lived here and he spent the rest of the ride complaining about City Hall.

"Do you live here?" Patsy asked him as we got out of the cab.

"Nah!" he said. "I live in Brooklyn."

I never go to the U.N. without stopping first on the sidewalk to feast my eyes on the original buildings—the Secretariat and the General Assembly— with the hundred-odd member-nation flags flying in front of them. The U.N. occupies sixteen acres of land (mostly donated by the Rockefellers) and the years have seen the addition of a U.N. Library building, Dag Hammarskjöld Plaza and the Eleanor Roosevelt Memorial. Across the way, we saw the construction mess which, by the time you read this, will have opened as One U.N. Plaza, New York's newest luxury-hotel and office building, in sloping blue-green glass.

As we got our tickets at the tour desk, I looked up at the Foucault Pendulum swinging above the grand staircase and told Patsy:

"Every time I come here, I make up my mind that this time I'll understand how that thing gives me 'visible proof of the rotation of the Earth,' as it claims in the booklet. And every time I come here, I don't."

"If you come here early in the morning, the pendulum will be swinging one way," said Patsy, "and if you come back late in the afternoon it'll be swinging the opposite way. And you know the pendulum didn't turn around, so the Earth must have turned around."

"Thank you," I said. "It pays to go to Harvard," and we joined the tour.

Every time you go to the U.N., you see something new. Every new country admitted to membership presents a gift to the U.N. We hadn't been there since the admission of the People's Republic of China and our tour started with a look at China's spectacular gift. On a table almost the length of a wall stood a replica of a railroad system winding through the mountains and cities of China, done entirely in hand-carved ivory, with every tree, house and inch of track intricately detailed.

Every time you take the tour you also learn something new. The young guides have fifty times as much information in their heads as they can convey in a one-hour tour, and each guide is free to choose which features of each room and which art works to tell you about. The guides, drawn from all the U.N. countries, speak perfect English and are awesomely well informed.

"How do you know so much? How do you remember it all?" Patsy asked the attractive young woman from Sweden who was our guide; and the guide told us that all U.N. guides are required to attend a daily briefing on current debates and keep abreast of all the literature dealing with "the Economic and Social Council's seven thousand projects, the

UNESCO projects on behalf of children in one hundred countries and the administrative work of the Trusteeship Council."

Unless a meeting is going on in one of them, the tour takes you into all the main rooms—the Security Council chamber, the General Assembly hall and the meeting rooms of the Trusteeship Council and the Economic and Social Council. They're still the most beautifully designed and constructed assembly rooms I've ever been in.

At the end of the tour, you're deposited in the basement, free to spend time and money in the U.N. Bookstore, Gift Shop and Souvenir Shop. The unique feature of the bookstore is its English translations of children's books from all the U.N. countries. And don't buy ordinary souvenirs in ordinary shops till you've seen the U.N. souvenir and gift shops. The shipments of gift items from member nations are continuous and unpredictable. One month you'll find Israeli jewelry and African wood carving, the next month silk scarves from India and moccasins from Iceland.

Patsy got carried away by all the exotica and bought a set of cushions labeled "Four Peas in a Pod": four round green cushions shaped like peas, fitted into a long, split green cushion shaped like a pod.

Made in Vermont.

Even if you're not nostalgic about Hollywood, you have got to take the Rockefeller Center tour, the highlight of which is a tour of Radio City Music Hall, the supercolossal zenith of movie palaces.

(The NBC strike hadn't ended, we'd just got tired of waiting. When it was finally settled, we went back and took the NBC tour and found it dull. Since television production is based in Hollywood, the NBC tour was confined to looking through glass windows at news rooms, soap-opera stages and the studios of NBC's local radio station. The only mild diversions were a demonstration of old-time radio sound effects and a chance to walk onto a TV stage and see yourself on a monitor.)

"Rockefeller Center" originally meant the group of low buildings clustered around the central seventy-story RCA Building, fronting Fifth Avenue at Forty-ninth Street and extending to Sixth Avenue. Today the Center has grown to a mammoth complex of some twenty-odd buildings (they keep adding) mushrooming west from Fifth past Sixth almost to Seventh. The main buildings are connected by an underground concourse, and if you can find your way through the concourse—which mostly you can't— you can go from building to building and see most of the Center's 200 shops, 26 restaurants and 18 banks without ever going out in the rain.

But to most New Yorkers, "Rockefeller Center" still means the original grouping, and you can see it best from across the street outside the doors of Saks: a group of buildings of graduated heights set round a green plaza with the RCA Building ("30 Rock") rising in the background. Cross the avenue to the Center and walk through the plaza and you'll see a sunken plaza below it. The lower level is an ice-skating rink in winter and an out-door restaurant in summer; on the upper level there's a kind of kibitzers' balcony from which to stare down at the skaters or diners, an essential amenity in a city where People-Watching is a favorite sport.

"Did you know," I said to Patsy as we waited in the RCA lobby for the tour to start, "that when Rockefeller Center first opened, it caused as much outrage as the World Trade Center? It opened in the thirties, and everybody said the city didn't need a huge office complex in the middle of a Depression."

"Where'd you read that?" Patsy asked skeptically.

"They said," I continued, "that nobody'd rent enough office space to pay for the upkeep, nobody had the money to open shops, and nobody could afford to buy in them if they did open. And they said Who needed a movie palace seating sixty-two hundred people, when every neighborhood movie theater had to give away dishes to lure families into buying tickets?"

"Who told you all that?" Patsy demanded.

"Cole Porter even wrote a line about it in a song," I said. "Sung by Fred Astaire. Nobody told me. I remember it. I was going to school in Philadelphia and I read about it in the *Evening Bulletin*."

123

28. ROCKEFELLER PLAZA
*Above the skating rink, the Kibitzers' Balcony;
above that, a kibitzers' railing at street level.*

29. ROCKEFELLER PLAZA AT CHRISTMAS.
The tree stands in front of "30 Rock."

Patsy was regarding me with detached interest.

"You must be ninety!" she said pleasantly.

The tour took us through the RCA Building first, and we stopped at a small, unlikely garden built outside the seventh-floor windows and visible only from the upper floors of the building we were in and the upper floors of nearby office buildings.

"This garden is never used," the guide told us. "It is here for the psychological relief of office workers on high floors."

We were also, of course, taken to the seventieth-floor observation roof with its marvelous skyline views. Which reminds me: if you can't get a reservation at Windows on the World (the World Trade Center restaurant), the next best place from which to see New York at night is the Rainbow Room on the sixty-fifth floor of the RCA Building. BUT BE WARY: unlike Windows on the World, the Rainbow Room has tables at narrow corner windows with almost no view. If you're stuck at one of these, get up and walk to the nearest broad window before you leave, and look out and see what Thomas Edison and New York's anonymous architects have wrought in the way of an incandescent miracle.

We went through the concourse and into the lobbies of the famous original buildings: the Italian Building, with Atlas holding up the world on its façade; and the French and British buildings—and I would have been just as happy if the guide hadn't told us that the plaza gardens are officially named the Channel Gardens because they have the French building at one end and the British at the other.

From there, we proceeded to Sixth Avenue to the Largest Indoor Theater in the World, containing the Largest Indoor Stage in the World, Radio City Music Hall.

The tour began in the great lobby, from which we descended a sweeping staircase to the lounge, a full city block long, thickly carpeted and furnished with chairs and sofas, and ceiling and wall decorations in the grand Hollywood style.

"Do you remember a ladies' room here where the toilet seat sprang up and glowed with violet light when you rose from it?" I asked Patsy. "Ultraviolet disinfectant was common for a while later on, but at the time no other toilet in town lit up lavender and it unnerved me."

"No, the one I remember," she said, "had mirrored walls on all sides. It was terrifying: you not only saw yourself from all angles but on into infinity."

The tour guide's talk was entirely devoted to weights-and-measures: how many feet wide and high the stage was, how many tons of cable it took to raise the whale-sized orchestra from the pit to the stage on an electronic platform; how many acres of seats the theater's vast tiers held; how many tons the World's Largest Indoor Organ weighed.

(The plans for the Music Hall were drawn up in 1929, when organ music accompanied silent films; and either the management was already stuck with the World's Largest Organ when the theater opened, or didn't think the talkies would last.)

Patsy and I moved away from the tour group to wallow in our memories of Radio City Music Hall stage shows. And if I speak of them in the past tense, it's less because the Music Hall may have been converted to other forms of entertainment by the time you come than because the place itself is so firmly part of a long-gone past for both of us.

Traditionally, New Yorkers have gone to Radio City Music Hall only at three stages in their lives: (1) when they were children; (2) when they were young and dating; (3) when they had children of their own to take to the annual Christmas or Easter or Fourth of July extravaganza. Patsy, who grew up in New York, was awash with memories of the annual Christmas show, which had been the high point of every childhood year:

"First the lights went down and you'd hear the organ. You wouldn't see it, you'd just hear it. Then a purple light would come up over on the side, and you'd see the organ and the organist sliding slowly out of the wall in a purple glow. Then, while the organist played, you had to wait—the wait was absolutely endless because you were so excited—for the show to begin. Then, while the organist was still playing, you'd look up at the side boxes and they'd be full of biblical statues. And then, slowly, the statues would move, and you'd see they were people, and they'd come down from the boxes and march slowly up the side aisles and onto the stage. They were marching," she explained, "to Bethlehem. And then a star would appear and lead everybody to the manger for the big tableau."

Then the hundred-and-fifty-piece orchestra rose slowly up out of the pit and the stage show began.

"First came the acrobats, who threw each other around," said Patsy, "and then the men with the animal acts, who threw the animals around. I always worried for fear one of the dogs would Make, right there on the stage. And then the soloist—it was always some terrible singer—would sing Christmas carols. And then came the ballet. And finally, just as you thought you'd die if they didn't come soon, the Rockettes. And they were wonderful."

All Radio City Music Hall stage shows followed that format. They were all spectacles, sumptuously costumed and performed against a background of half a ton of resplendent scenery.

"Did you ever see the Fourth of July show, with the electronic fireworks going off at the end?" Patsy asked me. "The Rockettes wore red-white-and-blue sequin shorts and sequin tap shoes and sequin Uncle Sam vests, and they all snapped their heads to the left at the same second and when they went *tap,*-ta-ta-*tap,* ta-ta-*tap-tap-tap,* every knee was in an exact line with every other knee. And four hundred men would march down from

128

the boxes in sequin Uncle Sam suits and sequin stovepipe Uncle Sam hats, singing 'You're a Grand Old Flag'—and the electric fireworks would go off and make a huge flag for the final tableau." And she added thoughtfully, "It was so terrible it was remarkable."

I'll tell you an old joke that will sum up Radio City Music Hall for you.

It seems a man and his wife went to the Music Hall one Sunday afternoon, arriving toward the end of the film. When it ended, the house lights came up for a few minutes before the stage show and the man rose, murmuring to his wife:

"I'm going to the men's room."

He located an exit on his floor—orchestra, loge, mezzanine, balcony or second balcony—but he couldn't find a men's room on it. He descended a staircase and looked on the next floor and couldn't find a men's room and descended another staircase. He walked along corridors and pushed open doors, he went along dark passages and up and down steps, getting more and more lost and more and more frantic. Just as his need became intolerably urgent, he pushed open a heavy door and found himself on a small street lined with houses, trees and shrubs. There was no one in sight and the man relieved himself in the bushes.

All this had taken time, and it took him additional time to work his way back up to his own floor and locate his own aisle and section. By the time he finally reached his seat, the stage show had ended and the movie had begun again. The man slid into his seat, whispering to his wife:

"How was the stage show?"

To which his wife replied:

"You ought to know. You were in it."

We came out on Sixth Avenue—and maybe because the Music Hall had evoked the past so vividly, we both looked at the avenue with new eyes. The transformation of midtown Sixth Avenue over the past ten

129

or fifteen years has been extraordinary. Back in the fifties it was one long honky-tonk row of shooting galleries, cheap souvenir shops, third-rate secondhand bookstores and dingy cafeterias. Today, from Forty-eighth to Fifty-ninth Street, Sixth Avenue is so opulent a row of office towers set in landscaped plazas that if you put a few flags and trees around, you could almost start calling it the Avenue of the Americas. The best time to see it is early in the evening when you're on your way to a Broadway theater. At dusk every skyscraper is blazing with light, the plazas are illuminated and walking down the avenue is dazzling.

We had lunch at a Japanese restaurant near the Music Hall; and not till we'd worked our way through both tempura and sukiyaki and the waitress had brought our second pot of tea, did I push across the table to Patsy a typewritten itinerary for Blockbuster Sunday:

> St. Mark's-in-the-Bouwerie
> The Lower East Side (Orchard St.)
> Chinatown
> City Hall
> Wall Street-on-a-Sunday
> Trinity churchyard.

Patsy didn't bat an eye. She just shot me a sidelong glance and asked:
"Why did you leave it off?"
"Well, I did think about it," I said, "because we did go on a very cloudy day, the visibility was only five miles, and I thought I'd wait and see, and if it's very clear on Sunday—"
"You know we're going back up there," said Patsy, and added "W.T.C." to the bottom of the list.

We poured ourselves more tea and lit cigarettes. Then Patsy, staring into her teacup somberly, said:
"Do you realize what we owe the Rockefellers?" And she ticked the

130

30. ROCKEFELLER UNIVERSITY
graduates Ph.D.'s in the sciences.

debt off on her fingers. "The Cloisters. Riverside Church. Lincoln Center. Rockefeller Center. The U.N.—"

"Rockefeller University," I said. "It's around the corner from me. It's beautiful." Rockefeller University is a scientific graduate school, it graduates only Ph.D.'s. "I read somewhere that its faculty has won nine Nobel prizes in the last five years."

"From the top of this island to the bottom," said Patsy soberly, "and from the East River to the Hudson with Rockefeller Center in the middle, we owe them so much!"

"Harry Truman would tell you that the Rockefeller fortune was built on the blood of Colorado miners," I said.

"I know, I read Merle Miller's book, too," said Patsy. "I know it's blood money."

"Still—" I said.

Patsy nodded.

To the Rockefellers, living and dead, whose blood money has so greatly enriched the landscape of New York City and the lives of New Yorkers:

Thanks for everything.

Once upon a time, when this city was the Dutch town of New Amsterdam, a new governor arrived from Holland named Peter Stuyvesant. He was a moral man and choleric, and he took a fit at what he found here: one unfinished church, one unfinished school, fifty decaying houses and seventeen taprooms.

Peter Stuyvesant went to work and over the next two decades transformed the town into an orderly and prosperous community of houses, farms and shipyards. He was a bad-tempered man with a dictatorial manner; he stumped around town on his peg leg, quarreling with everybody. He was also a bigot who wanted to ship all the Quakers to Rhode Island. ("They have all sorts of riffraff people there," he explained.) Every now and then, the Staats General sent him peremptory orders to stop harassing minorities.

Stuyvesant built himself a large farm along the East River—a *bouwerie,* as the Dutch called it—where for twenty-four years he lived the good life of an autocratic governor. Then, in 1664, the Duke of York's troops invaded New Amsterdam. Knowing that resistance would get him nothing but a bombed city and slaughtered inhabitants, Stuyvesant surrendered without firing a shot. The Duke of York, not content with renaming the entire province of New Netherlands "New York province" after himself, also named the city after himself. New Amsterdam became New York City and Dutch rule came to an end.

Stuyvesant was seventy-two years old by then, and the Staats General in Holland sent him a kind letter saying, in effect, "You've earned a peaceful retirement. Come on home."

And Peter Stuyvesant wrote back, saying, in effect, "I am home."

Whether you called it New Amsterdam or New York, this was his town. What was it to him if (like millions to follow) he had come here from somewhere else? Peter Stuyvesant withdrew to his *bouwerie* and lived out his old age as a private citizen of the city he had governed for twenty-four years. He died peacefully at home, and was buried in a vault in the family church.

Stuyvesant's farm and church are long gone. But a church was later built on the property, in that part of it which is still called the Bowery. And it was at this church—St. Mark's-in-the-Bouwerie, at Tenth Street and Second Avenue—that Patsy and I met, that Sunday morning, to pay our respects to the first New Yorker.

What we had gone there to see, we found in a side wall of the church: an old stone vault with an inscription which read:

In this vault lies buried
PETRUS STUYVESANT
Captain General and Governor-in-Chief of
New Amsterdam in New Netherlands
now called New York,
and the Dutch West-India Islands
died Feb. 4, A.D. 1672
Aged 80 years

"I have suppressed my poor-man's-historian instincts on other tours," I told Patsy as we left the churchyard, "but today we're doing Old New York. Here and there I just may remember a fascinating historical note which I will want to share with you."

"After talking my ears off about Peter Stuyvesant for half an hour, did you think you had to tell me that?" said Patsy.

We walked down along the Bowery and found the sidewalks empty on both sides of the avenue.

"Not a bum in sight," I said. And Patsy said reasonably:

"I guess, like everybody else, Bowery bums sleep late on Sunday."

We walked down to Houston Street (pronounced How-ston instead of Hew-ston, no book I ever read could tell me why), where the Lower East Side officially begins. But we had to walk on down to Orchard Street to see the real Sunday action.

The Orthodox Jews of the Lower East Side shut their shops early on Friday afternoon for the Sabbath, and reopen them on Sunday morning. And if you think the street scenes in the movie *Hester Street* depicted a bygone era, go down to Orchard Street on a sunny Sunday morning and correct your impression.

The street was closed to traffic when we got there, and a large banner strung across the street from the tops of tenements proclaimed: "ORCHARD STREET MALL." On Orchard Street, the word "mall" is about as appropriate as it would be for a street market in downtown Calcutta. We joined a dense mob of people inching along the middle of the street, looking to left and right at the merchandise jamming every inch of sidewalk on both sides of the street.

There were long racks of women's dresses and men's and women's pants, and graduated wooden platforms stuffed with rows of shoes and hats. Sandwiched between the racks and platforms were mountains of T-shirts and ties, piled on pieces of blanket spread on the sidewalk. Down the street we passed heavier racks with thick bolts of upholstery fabric, dress wools, and opulent rolls of gold and silver brocade positively blinding in the sun.

But that was only on the sidewalks in front of the shops. The shop owners obviously felt the need of more display space. Men's shirts on wire hangers hung from awnings and from the fire-escape railings of every tenement. Dresses on hangers hung from flagpoles, handbags hung from hooks driven into the brick walls, and a couple of hundred T-shirts dangled from a clothesline strung along an entire block of third-story tenement windows. In the dizzying welter of merchandise cramming the sidewalks and hanging in midair from every available anchorage, the shops themselves—where uptown New Yorkers buy designer clothes at half price—were almost invisible.

A woman was coming toward us, pushing her way expertly through the solid sea of bodies in the center of the "mall" and passing out handbills as she came. We took one. Under the name and address of the store, the handbill advertised:

PARIS IMPORTS
Yves Saint Laurent   Valentino   Pierre Cardin
Gucci   Pierre D'Alby   Anne Klein
Calvin Klein   French Jeans

"Tell them," said Patsy as I wrote all this down, "the difference between Sunday and Monday. You come down here Sunday to sightsee; you come down Monday-through-Thursday to shop."

When we came abreast of Fine & Klein, the most famous of the cut-rate clothing stores on Orchard Street, we inched our way over to the sidewalk to look at the Gucci bags and Cardin suits in the window, and I saw what Patsy meant. The store was so jammed with shoppers that an employe stood in the doorway barring entrance to any more customers till some of those inside departed.

This is how you shop down there. Go to a Fifth Avenue store and find the Cacharel suit or Hermès bag you want. Copy down the number on the tag and take the number with you to Orchard Street. Designer clothes are never on display on the sidewalk, and only a few are displayed in the shops themselves. Most of them are kept packed away in boxes. But produce the number of the item you want, and the difference between the Fifth Avenue and Orchard Street prices will stagger you.

We passed two stores, close together, which were testimony to the overlapping neighborhoods around us. One was the A-ONE NACHAS KNIT SWEATER SHOP. (*Nachas* is the Yiddish word for "joy," so if you want an A-1 sweater knit with joy, that's where you'll find it.) The other was a religious artifacts store, its windows crammed with Catholic statues and medallions and an assortment of Christmas crèches. The older generation of Middle European Jews still clings to the Lower East Side; older Italians still cling to adjacent Little Italy; and below both, new waves of Hong Kong immigrants cling to overcrowded Chinatown. And the extent to which the three neighborhoods spill over into each other is visible on Sunday on Orchard Street. We saw boys wearing yarmulkas eating Italian ices, and Jewish and Chinese men deep in conversation. If you're here in September during the biggest of the city's Italian street fairs, the San Gennaro Festival on Mulberry Street, you'll see more Chinese than Italian faces looking down at the fair from tenement windows. And you won't believe it, but on Allen Street there's a kosher Chinese restaurant where the Chinese waiters wear yarmulkas. The truth is that the faces you see down there would stick out like sore thumbs in Rome or the Warsaw Ghetto or Hong Kong; they aren't Italian, Jewish and Chinese faces, they're New York faces.

We walked all the way down Orchard Street to Canal. We had passed famous Lower East Side streets at intersections all the way down. I managed to control myself as we crossed Rivington Street, famous for its huge sidewalk barrels of kosher pickles. But one block below Rivington, we came to Delancey Street.

"Did I ever tell you about Oliver De Lancey, the Outlaw of the Bronx?" I asked Patsy.

"Oh, God," said Patsy.

"He was a sort of commando raider," I said. "The De Lanceys were rich Tories, their sons were educated in England and so forth. Well, during the Revolution the De Lancey men became officers in the King's Loyal American regiment and fought bravely for the King's cause and they were all due to be knighted after England won the war. So was Jimmy Rivington. He published the Tory newspaper in New York during the British occupation. The British thought very highly of Jimmy, he was presented to the Prince of Wales when the Prince came to New York. Jimmy Rivington and the De Lancey men all expected to be among the first American Knights of the British Empire. Instead of which, they wound up giving their names to the two most famous lower-class immigrant streets in the world."

"Write that down," said Patsy automatically.

At Canal Street, we turned west to Mott, one of Chinatown's narrow main streets, clotted with restaurants, vegetable markets, curio shops, a Chinese bookstore, all of them on the ground floors of appallingly ancient, decayed tenements, but with a new modern Chinese Community Center rising hopefully in the middle of the block.

Since 1963, when American immigration laws were finally amended to include "Orientals," overcrowding in Chinatown has become more and more severe. A *Times* story identified Confucius Plaza as a publicly financed housing project, and to walk along Mott Street is to see how desperately it's needed.

It was nearly two o'clock by the time we got there and we were both ravenous; but as far as I'm concerned, there's no better street in New York for handling an appetite. The new Hong Kong immigrants of the sixties brought their Szechuan cuisine with them. They opened restaurants in Chinatown, to which New Yorkers who like hot food—chili-pepper hot—became addicted. As the immigrants learned enough English to move up-town, Szechuan restaurants sprang up in all New York neighborhoods; but walking along Mott Street, I happened to see the first Szechuan restaurant I'd ever tried and which I remembered with special pleasure.

"Do you like Szechuan food?" I asked Patsy.

"I like all Chinese food," said Patsy innocently.

"Well, I haven't been there in a long time," I said, "but Mandarin Inn used to be wonderful. Shall we try it?"

"Why not?" said Patsy. And we crossed the street to Mandarin Inn, where a sign in the hall informed us that Chef Wong demonstrated the preparation of lemon chicken on the second Sunday afternoon of every month. We didn't wait around for the demonstration, but we ordered the lemon chicken, and shrimp with garlic sauce, which were the Specialties of the Day. I ordered a side dish of Szechuan string beans from memory.

"Do you want your shrimp starred?" I asked Patsy as the waiter took our order.

"What do you mean?" she said.

"When a dish is starred or has a red check next to it, it means it's extra hot," I said. "Do you like hot spicy food?"

"No," said Patsy.

"It figured," I said. So I ordered my shrimp hot, she ordered hers mild. The lemon chicken is always mild, but I forgot to warn Patsy about the string beans. Being deep green, they looked cool. Patsy speared one, dropped it negligently into her mouth, and then began to claw the air. She

139

drank her glass of water, and mine, and a cup of tea before she managed, still gasping, to push the dish of string beans over to my side of the table.

I liked the lemon chicken better than the highly touted version served at a fashionable uptown restaurant where it's so saturated with sugar you can't taste the lemon.

"In my extremely limited experience," I said to Patsy, "every overpriced, super-chic restaurant in New York, where you can't get a table unless they Know you, turns out to have disappointing food when you finally get there. Whereas every neighborhood in New York has good, unpretentious restaurants where they'll feed you just as well, for half the price and none of the aggravation."

"Tourists should do what we did at Columbia," said Patsy. "Ask somebody going by on the street, 'Where's a good place to eat around here?'"

So you do that. Don't stop a man with a briefcase, he's probably a commuter. Wait till a man or woman comes along with groceries, a bike, a baby coach or a dog and ask him-or-her to recommend a restaurant.

We walked down Mulberry Street after lunch and passed a Chinese Teahouse and Pastry Shop. I had Sunday brunch in one of those shops once. Trays of hot filled pastry puffs were brought to the table, the pastries on one tray stuffed with shrimp, others with meat and vegetables, with a tray of sweet puffs for dessert.

On Mulberry as on Mott Street, the vegetable stores were open on Sunday, and through the open doorways we could see bok toy, the mustardy lettuce, fresh ginger and black, hundred-day-old duck eggs.

Ahead of us, at the end of Mulberry Street, rose the first towers of Lower Manhattan and we walked on west to City Hall at the upper end of the old city. On a deserted Sunday you can appreciate the grace of the low white building, its colonial columns and portico and domed clock

31. CITY HALL
*Behind the window under the clock sits the little man
with the encyclopedic head.*

tower tranquilly at home among the skyscrapers, thanks to City Hall Park, which keeps them at a respectful distance.

"You see that turret window up there on top?" I said, pointing up at the small window under the clock tower.

"What about it?" said Patsy.

"There's a little man who sits up there by himself in an office behind that window," I said. "He's been sitting up there for forty years and he's a human encyclopedia of New York City. Anybody in the City Administration who needs a New York fact or date or place-name origin, phones the little man up in that turret. He's been sitting up there through eight or nine administrations with his encyclopedic head; every mayor finds him indispensable and he outlasts them all."

City Hall Park being the center of a radius of Lower Manhattan streets, we had to decide which exit would take us down to Trinity Church. Patsy studied several YOU ARE HERE maps and then informed me that they were all upside down, but that Broadway should take us down to Wall Street. We crossed an empty, silent intersection and started down Broadway into the financial district.

The absolute quiet and emptiness of Lower Manhattan on a Sunday spreads it out before you like a model city, giving you a chance to see it first in perspective and then, as you walk, in a series of small, clear-cut pictures.

At the corner of Broadway and Liberty, in the shadow of the huge Marine Midland building, Patsy clutched my arm and said:

"Look down there!"

And I looked down a long curving canyon as dramatic as Wall Street's.

32. WALL STREET ON A SUNDAY
At 10:30 A.M. by the Trinity clock.

33. THAMES STREET BRIDGE

At the next corner, Thames Street, she seized my arm again and ordered:

"Look up!"

On opposite corners of a narrow alley, two buildings rose maybe forty stories above the street, and on what might have been the thirty-fifth floor, a footbridge connected the two buildings. Somebody obviously got tired of taking an elevator all the way down, crossing the narrow alley and taking another elevator all the way up, and built a bridge outside two thirty-fifth-floor windows to save steps.

We went on down to Wall Street, and there was Trinity Church, with the churchyard gate standing open. We found Hamilton's impressive monument, and Gallatin's, and what I consider a fitting monument to Robert Fulton: an enormous, pretentious tomb—but empty. (His remains are buried elsewhere.) And we came upon a gravestone which touched me very much.

The stone must have been recently restored, because the legend on it was plain and easy to read from the outside path on which we stood. What touched me, however, was not what was on the stone but what I could read between the lines.

The inscription noted that the deceased had been a "merchant of New York" until 1783, when he had "removed to Newfoundland where he established a new home," and where he had died fifteen years later.

"I promise I won't bore you with any more stories if you'll just listen to this one," I told Patsy. "First read the stone."

Patsy read it and then asked obligingly:

"Who was he?"

"I don't know. Nobody. Just a merchant," I said. "But he was a Tory. 1783 was the year when the British left New York, after seven years of occupation. They left in November, and most Tories left at the same time. Some of them were afraid of reprisals from the returning patriots, and

145

some of them just didn't want to live under a rebel government; they wanted to stay English. So England offered them free passage to Newfoundland, and they became pilgrims all over again, sailing off to another wilderness—in winter—to start a new life. Well, here's one of them. He 'removed to Newfoundland and established a new home there' and died there. Only he must have left instructions in his will for his body to be carried, by ship, all the way back to New York to be buried in Trinity churchyard—because here he is."

"That's a nice story for a book about New York," said Patsy judiciously. "Use that."

It was after four when we left the churchyard. We had been walking steadily since ten that morning. My shoes hated two of my toes and a bone in my right foot; Patsy's kept mutinously dropping off behind her. But it was a sunny day and, in the absence of exhaust fumes, the air was sharply clear. The World Trade Center towers looked closer than they were and we pushed on toward them without bothering to discuss it. If you're gung-ho about New York, and you're that close to that view on a bright, clear day, you're going back up there whether your feet want to or not. But we were very thankful when our feet finally made it to the World Trade Center entrance and we walked into the surrealistic lobby. Then we looked up at the mezzanine.

The line of people waiting to buy tickets ran clear around the mezzanine; everybody in New York had discovered it was a clear day. But the sign on the ticket window said, "View to the Horizon," and we'd passed the point of no return anyway, so we went all the way around the mezzanine and got on the end of the line, where we stood, inching along, for twenty-five minutes. Then one of the two elevators took us up, and we sat in one window seat after another gawking out and down in blissful silence, the long wait forgotten.

"If it were six instead of five," said Patsy, "we'd be able to watch the sunset."

"Does this building face west?" I asked.

"It faces everywhere," said Patsy positively. "It does everything."

When we'd sat in every window seat, we finally rose to leave. And I don't know why it didn't occur to us that if two elevators took twenty-five minutes to get all of us up there, they would take at least that long to get all of us back down. Standing on line all over again, I was getting a backache and I leaned backwards to relieve it. Whereupon Patsy inquired:

"What are you doing?"

"I have a backache," I said.

"That's not what you do for a backache," said Patsy. "Bend forward with your arms stretched out and then bend down till you touch the floor."

I leaned over and, as my fingertips touched the floor, a hand began thumping my head down to meet them.

"Relax your head," advised Patsy. Which is how I discovered that your head is not like your arms or legs, you can't relax it, or stiffen it, you can't do anything with it. Like Mount Everest, it's just there. And all this time, Patsy's two hands industriously pushing my head down and Patsy's voice commanding authoritatively:

"Relax your head."

How we looked to the rest of the line it didn't occur to us to consider; we were too busy with what we were doing.

By the time we got back down to the ground floor, we were so tired I needed a new definition of the word. Patsy supplied it.

We had a long subway ride still ahead of us, and we had to locate our separate subways through a network of unfinished corridors. Before embarking on this final lap, I fished out my cigarettes and lit one. Patsy usually prefers her own brand but she was just standing, swaying slightly, staring at my pack in a kind of vacant stupor.

"You want a cigarette?" I asked—and took one of mine out of the pack and extended it to her. Patsy stared at it a moment.

"No," she said finally. "I wouldn't have the strength to draw on it."

That's tired.

*   *   *

I didn't hear from Patsy till Wednesday evening.

"I've been paralyzed for three days," she said when she phoned. "Both the shoes I wore Sunday have holes in them."

"Don't complain to me, I've got two corns and a bunion," I said.

"Well, you told me to save Thursday," said Patsy, "but I'm warning you: I'm only up to something very easy and midtown."

"So am I," I said—and wondered how to tell her what I had in mind.

"Okay," said Patsy. "As long as we don't have to do it this week, I'll tell you why I called you. There's a black-owned sightseeing bus company that does a three-hour tour of Harlem. We have to reserve seats in advance. You want me to call them and book seats for next week?"

"Fine," I said. "Any day you can make, I can make."

"Right," said Patsy—and couldn't resist adding: "Guess where their first stop is?"

"Where?" I said.

"The Jumel mansion," said Patsy. "I told you we'd see everything! Now, what's for tomorrow?"

"We'll only need a couple of hours," I said cautiously. "You want to meet me at Bloomingdale's at three?"

"I don't like Bloomingdale's," said Patsy.

"I went to Zabar's; you can go to Bloomingdale's," I said. "Meet me at the Lexington Avenue entrance."

Considering our mutual fear of heights, I saw no reason to tell her in advance that I considered it our duty as tourists to get on a cable car suspended over midtown Manhattan and ride across the East River and back on it.

A few blocks from where I live, there's a pedestrian walk along the river, above the East River Drive. If you're strolling along it, you'll see on the opposite bank a small island, two miles long, running parallel with the East Side from Forty-second Street to Seventy-ninth.

The city bought the island from a man named Blackwell back in 1823 and for years it was known as Blackwell's Island, but in the twentieth century it became better known as Welfare Island because of the free hospitals-for-incurables the city built and maintained there. (In the early years of the century the island also had a very jazzy jail. Boss Tweed had "a magnificent cell" there, according to the brochure, with a picture window to give him a view of the city he'd robbed blind. And Mae West spent ten days there for appearing in a play she wrote called *Sex*.)

By the early sixties, when I first became aware of it, Welfare Island was occupied only by two hospitals for the severely handicapped. The hospitals had large, permanent populations and the patients were citizens with voting rights. And since Welfare Island ran parallel with our neighborhood, it was included in the assembly district represented by our local Democratic club. So during every political campaign, our club leaders climbed into a car, with our state assembly or city council candidate in the back seat, and drove across the Queensboro Bridge, and then back through part of Queens, to visit the voters on Welfare Island. The trip took fifteen minutes without traffic, thirty minutes with traffic.

This year the club leaders drove over as usual; but they saw ten times as many voters as ever before and they probably made the trip by car for the last time. Because this year, the island has been transformed; it is now Roosevelt Island, a new suburb built to house 2,200 families in small apartment houses (small for New York, at least). And the island's residents will commute to New York not in fifteen to thirty minutes, but in four. A tramway has been built to carry them back and forth across the East River by cable car, for the price of a subway token. The tram made its first run last Monday.

The cable cars leave from a specially constructed depot above Sixtieth Street and Second Avenue. Which is why I told Patsy to meet me at Bloomingdale's. Bloomingdale's occupies a square block from Fifty-ninth to Sixtieth and from Lexington to Third. But if I'd told Patsy to meet me on the Third Avenue side, she might have got there before I did; she might have looked toward Second and seen the tramway depot—and guessed—and bolted. So we met at the Lexington Avenue entrance to Bloomingdale's.

"Put this in your shoulder bag, but don't forget to read it later, it's funny," said Patsy, handing me the inevitable clipping.

152

"Why don't you like Bloomie's?" I asked as we went into the store where I was going to walk her through to the Third Avenue exit.

"It's too big," said Patsy. "I can't find anything."

"If you just remember that Bloomingale's was once a cheap department store on Lexington Avenue," I said, "that's all you need to know—because it's still, basically speaking, a cheap department store *on Lexington Avenue*. When the Third Avenue El came down and Third Avenue became beautiful and expensive, Bloomingdale's naturally added a beautiful and expensive Third Avenue side. So you take the Lexington Avenue escalator up to the cheap-clothes floors, and the Third Avenue escalator up to the designer-clothes floor. But they have a great furniture department, a great housewares department and a sensational gourmet food shop in the basement, so don't say you don't like it."

By this time, we had come out on Third Avenue, Patsy following me absent-mindedly. But as we started walking toward Second, she saw the new tramway depot looming overhead at the corner of Second, and stopped cold.

"We're not going up in that ski lift!" she said.

"We owe it to my readers," I said.

I kept on walking and she followed me in silence. At the corner of Second Avenue a flight of stone steps led up to the tramway platform. We reached the foot of the steps and Patsy halted again. She waved an arm toward the cable wire overhead.

"Do you see what you're going to be riding on?" she demanded. "It's a piece of string!"

"I couldn't do it alone," I said piously. "Together, we can do anything."

She followed me up the stone steps to the platform, where we stood and watched the cable car glide toward us from the island, swaying gently as it crossed the river.

"Will you look how it's shaking?" said Patsy. "Why do we have to try this thing the first week it's operating? They haven't got it safe yet!"

The car landed, and the people who stepped out of it were smiling, which gave me the courage to push Patsy into it ahead of me. We were joined by a dozen other thrill-seekers with nothing better to do in the middle of a Thursday afternoon.

The cable car, a glass bubble with standard bus seats, runs alongside the Queensboro Bridge, and since we were level with the cars going by on the bridge, we had no more sense of height than we'd have had in an ordinary El train. What we did have, as the car stood poised over midtown Manhattan at the edge of the river and then started slowly on its way, was a goggle-eyed view of present-day transportation.

Below us, on land, was the usual Second Avenue traffic jam of buses, trucks and cars. On the water were a couple of barges, a commuter's motorboat and a Circle Line sightseeing boat taking tourists on the time-honored trip around Manhattan island. Above us, planes flew in the distance, and as we crossed the river, a helicopter went by on its way to one of the airports.

And Patsy, who had been shaking when she stepped into it, was darting back and forth from one side of the car to the other, barking:

"Look down there! Look over here! Look out that way!"

The tramcar landed at the new suburb, unfinished and sparsely inhabited as yet, though the rental offices were busy. We walked nearly the length of it, admiring the small six-and-seven-story apartment houses, the new streets and park, the new school and swimming pool, a very old church and the old Blackwell house on its way to becoming a community center.

"It's pretty now, like a toy city," I said to Patsy. "But you can visualize the fast-food stores and parking lot, and they've already got space set

35. HOW TO COMMUTE FROM ROOSEVELT ISLAND

aside for the suburban shopping center. Riding a cable car over the East River is something tourists might want to try. But once they get here, all they'll see is one more standardized suburb."

(Two days later, riding a cable car over the East River turned out to be something half of New York wanted to try. On the tram's first weekend, twenty thousand New Yorkers converged on it, bringing their children and a picnic lunch, prepared for a day's outing on Roosevelt Island, which had no picnic facilities. The families picnicked all over it and, when the trash baskets overflowed, littered all over it. The island also had no public toilets, and the results of that were so horrendous that the beleaguered islanders threatened to close down the tramway if the weekend invasion continued. It didn't. Within two weeks, the novelty had worn off and the tram trip to Roosevelt Island joined the list of sightseeing tours New Yorkers are definitely going to take some day, like the trip to the Statue of Liberty.)

That afternoon when I got home, I dug Patsy's clipping out of my shoulder bag. It was from the *Times* and featured a photograph of Trinity churchyard and the intelligence that the graveyard had become a favorite lunchtime meeting place for young pot-smokers. I phoned Patsy.

"I forgot to tell you," she said. "We're booked for the Harlem tour at ten A.M. Monday. Penny Sightseeing Bus, 303 West Forty-second, write it down."

I wrote it down, and said:

"I read that clipping. Do you really think a story about pot-smoking in Trinity's graveyard belongs in a book for tourists?"

"It's a modern sidelight. Put it in," said Patsy. "Now listen. I've been thinking about that story you told me. About the Tory who left New York after the Revolution and fled to Buffalo."

156

"NEWFOUNDLAND," I said. Buffalo. I was losing all my respect for Harvard.

"Well, wherever it was," said Patsy. "What exactly did the stone say?"

I went and got my notes and came back and reported:

"I didn't take his name. What I took verbatim was that he was a 'merchant of New York who removed to Newfoundland in 1783 and established a new home there,' and I must have looked at the birth-and-death dates because I made note that he died up there fifteen years later."

"Was it a gravestone," asked Patsy, "or a plaque?"

"A gravestone, I think," I said.

"I think so, too, but you'll have to make sure," said Patsy. "Because it occurred to me: if it was a plaque, then he's buried in Newfoundland and somebody just put up the plaque in his memory."

"You've just ruined a beautiful story," I said. "But the lettering was very clear, I could read it easily from the outside path, so it might have been a plaque."

"Is it worth going back down to check it?" Patsy asked. "Or do you just want to phone them?"

"We have to go back down anyway," I said. "We still haven't toured the Stock Exchange."

"Oh, right," said Patsy. "And I want to check up on that bank; I want to see if they've put up a new wall plaque. All right, just put the Tory's gravestone on your list or we'll forget it."

As things turned out, we were to be in no danger of forgetting it. Ever.

This day started with a mystery, and Patsy and I aren't sure it didn't end with one.

We'd been having unnaturally hot weather and, a month earlier than usual, New York City was air-conditioned to death. To give you an example—and a warning: two friends of mine landed in hospitals with pneumonia, in July, from the icy, air-conditioned offices they worked in. I get frozen out of restaurants and movie theaters all summer; and since the buses to Jersey resorts always delivered me to the beach wih a sore throat and a sinus cough, I began to worry about the Harlem bus. On Saturday, therefore, I phoned the Penny Sightseeing Company. A man answered the phone.

"I'm booked for your Monday morning tour," I said, "and I wondered whether your bus is heavily air-conditioned and whether we'll need to bring sweaters."

And he said:

"You must be Mrs. Gibbs."

My mouth fell open.

"I'm coming with Mrs. Gibbs," I said.

"Oh, that's right," he said. "There are two of you. We do have one air-conditioned bus, but the air-conditioning doesn't work very well so it's never very cold."

I thanked him and we hung up; and I called Patsy. I told her that the man who answered the phone had said immediately, "You must be Mrs. Gibbs," and I went on:

"We must be the only passengers on the bus. Will you mind that?"

"No, it means we can ask a lot of questions," said Patsy.

We met in front of the bus office and went upstairs to the ticket office. There was a man behind the desk and he smiled and said good morning, and Patsy said:

"We have seats reserved on the ten o'clock bus."

And he said:

"You're Mrs. Gibbs."

But when we paid for our tickets, he got out a list of names and checked off ours at the bottom of a long list.

"The other passengers have gone downstairs to the bus stop," he said. "You'd better go right down; the bus'll be along any minute."

As we went downstairs, I said to Patsy:

"Maybe he knows we're the only whites on the bus."

We got down to the bus entrance and found the other passengers assembled on the sidewalk. There were thirty-five of them. All thirty-five were white.

"It's a Group," Patsy murmured. "We're the only ones not in the Group."

But we examined our fellow passengers furtively and, except for a couple here and a threesome there, they were obviously strangers to each other.

The bus arrived, the door opened, and as we filed onto the bus, the driver, who was also white, beamed at us and greeted us individually with "Good morning," and "Hello, how are you?"

We found seats and settled ourselves and I got out my notebook. Then the tour guide came aboard. The tour guide was a handsome, middle-aged man and the only black on the bus. As the bus pulled away and headed uptown, the guide said, in a resonant baritone voice:

"I want to welcome you, and to ask you to tell me whenever I'm going too fast for you. Mrs. Penny, the owner of the bus company, tells me you all speak English, but wherever we stop, there will be information sheets available in your own language. According to my list, you're all from Germany, France or Australia, but sometimes the list is incomplete, so if you need information sheets in some other language, just tell me."

The man I talked to on the phone had said, "You're Mrs. Gibbs," as soon as he heard my American accent. Patsy and I were the only Americans on the bus.

The guide told us he had been in show business for twenty years and that conducting sightseeing tours was something he did in his spare time.

"I do this because I enjoy it," he said. "I like Harlem and I enjoy showing it to people."

(The bus wasn't air-conditioned and as I sat happily by an open window, Patsy, perspiring freely, muttered in my ear, "Make a note: No Smoking, no john and no air-conditioning," and declined my offer to trade seats with her. "I don't want that hot air blowing on me," she said.)

The bus was rolling along Central Park West and the guide, who had been pointing out the sights along the way, suddenly paralyzed us by pointing to the building Patsy lives in.

"That is one of the city's finest old apartment houses," he announced, and added, "Steve Lawrence and Eydie Gormé live there."

"They moved out," Patsy hissed at me. "Should I tell him?"

"Have you got any celebrities to substitute?" I asked her.

"Margaret Mead?" suggested Patsy. "Abe Burrows? Helen Gurley Brown?"

"Fine," I said. "We'll tell him later."

The bus drove on up to 116th Street, where the guide pointed upward to a back-of-beyond view of the spires of St. John's Cathedral and part of the Columbia quadrangle, the buildings so far above us on a cliff we had to crane our necks to see them.

"Do you see where we were?" Patsy squeaked. "On that parapet? We had to be crazy!"

We were in Harlem now, driving through a neighborhood of sharp contrasts. On our left were huge modern housing projects with ground-floor playgrounds and landscaped walks; on our right, directly opposite the projects, rows of indescribably decayed and crumbling five-story brownstone tenements. But as we rolled on upward, past the graceful stone entrance gate to City College and then past the Grange, Alexander Hamilton's home, we were on a wide avenue driving through an attractive, middle-class Harlem neighborhood, where old shade trees on front lawns framed bay-windowed Victorian houses. We passed a modern Episcopal church building which the guide told us had been built by its black parishioners in 1970, after the old church building had burned down, and which had won a prize for its architect.

I was taking frantic notes on all this when Patsy turned to me abruptly and demanded:

"Why?"

"Why what?" I said.

"Why are we the only Americans on the bus?"

"I don't know," I said. "Maybe Americans don't know about the tour. I didn't."

"Then how did the foreigners find out about it?" said Patsy. "They can't all have read the fine print in the Convention & Visitors Bureau guide the way I did. I was looking through it to see if we'd missed anything or I'd never have known about it either."

The bus drew up outside the Morris-Jumel house, and as we piled out, I said to Patsy:

"When the guide isn't too busy, I'll ask him."

One of the curators met us at the door and she obviously knew the Penny operation well because she stood ready with mimeographed information sheets in German and French, and four in English for us and two young men from Australia.

The house was built before the Revolution by Roger Morris, a Tory, who abandoned it to emigrate to England. During the war it served as headquarters first for Washington, then for the British and finally for the Hessians; and the military documents and letters on display around the walls dealt mostly with the British-Hessian occupation. Years later the house was bought by a Frenchman named Jumel, whose chief claim to fame was that his widow was married to Aaron Burr for four months; and a few Burr portraits and letters were also on display, along with a great many Jumel possessions, none of them particularly interesting.

Patsy and I found the house and its contents dull; what the German and French tourists thought, we didn't know. When you're in a Revolutionary War museum and the only comments you hear around you are in French and German, you feel a little weird. So it was a relief when one of the Australians pointed to the date on a military despatch and said to his companion:

"That was the year Australia was first settled!"

Patsy and I went outside for a cigarette and a look at the view: the Jumel house is on a hill above the Harlem River. As we looked across the river to the woods drifting northward along the opposite bank, I said:

"That woods over there once belonged to a very sociable Dutch burgher named Jonas Bronck. He came to New Netherlands and bought a stretch of farmland over there and he built a big farm and a big farmhouse for his family. But they got bored living up there by themselves, and Jonas started inviting New Amsterdam families out to his place for a week or two. So you'd be walking along Wall Street or the docks, and you'd see a family piling their children and their clothes boxes into a boat and you'd ask them where they were going. And they'd say, 'We've been invited up to the mainland to visit the Broncks' or 'We're going up to see the Broncks.' I don't know who changed the *cks* to an *x*."

The guide came out with the rest of the tourists and led us all around the corner to a narrow street, a cul-de-sac two blocks long that was probably once a mews attached to the Jumel house. On both sides of the street were trim lines of small, upright houses with front steps that ran parallel with the sidewalk, rising to a landing where they turned a right angle to the front door. But you could only see the steps by walking around a barrier. In front of each house, a tall, left-handed triangle of brightly painted wood hid the steps and the landing from view. One barrier was dark green, one bright yellow, most were white. The line of houses with their

164

brightly painted shields seemed to have dropped into twentieth-century New York from another world.

"This street is Sylvan Terrace," the guide told us. "The houses are very expensive; only wealthy black families can afford them." And as he led the way back to the bus, he told the foreigners:

"There was a time when black New Yorkers had to live in Harlem because they were excluded from housing everywhere else. Now that they can live in other neighborhoods, when wealthy black families buy houses in Sylvan Terrace, it's because Harlem is where they want to live."

We drove along Edgecombe Avenue, an attractive residential street. Then we turned down Eighth Avenue and were abruptly on a depressed, dirty main street lined with shabby tenement storefronts. But as the bus approached 139th Street, the driver pointed to the block of it opening off Eighth Avenue.

"This block," he said, "and the next one—138th Street—are special. I want you to look at them."

We looked down 139th Street and saw a line of tall, handsome brownstones on a street that was scrupulously clean.

"These two blocks are very famous," said the guide. "They're called 'Strivers Row.' The houses were built by Stanford White, back at the turn of the century. The name 'Strivers Row' may have come from a West Indian named Striver who lived there. But the people of Harlem love their myths, and the Harlem folk tale is that the name comes from the fact that Strivers Row is where all the poor people of Harlem are striving to get. For years, Strivers Row had the only fine housing open to black people. The houses are still fine and they're still expensive. And like Sylvan Terrace, the Strivers Row houses are owned by people who don't have to live in Harlem but want to."

At 135th Street and Seventh Avenue, the foreigners heard the name of

37. "STRIVERS ROW" IN HARLEM
*From the house number, Patsy figured out scientifically
that this is the 138th Street block.*

Harlem's favorite son for the first time. At that corner, Seventh Avenue becomes Adam Clayton Powell Boulevard ("though they don't acknowledge the name-change downtown," the guide added drily). Powell was elected to Congress in 1944 and steadily re-elected until two years before his death in 1972. But he was also a preacher, and the bus made its second stop at the Abyssinian Baptist Church, which Powell made famous. At the height of his ministry, church membership stood at 18,000. Today it may still be the largest church congregation in the country with 12,000 members.

We were welcomed to the church by an aide to the minister, who gave us a brief history of it, pointed out the church's chief ornaments and then took us into the Powell Room, which might once have been a large social hall and is now a Powell museum. The photographs, plaques and testimonials, including one from the late Emperor Haile Selassie of Abyssinia (now Ethiopia), form a visual biography of Powell. He was a handsome man and the photographs of him are strikingly alive. More than that, they point up the singular fact of his life. Powell was expelled from Congress for precisely the same kind of political corruption for which a white senator had his wrist slapped by the same Congress in the same year. And the life of prejudice and hatred he endured, in and out of Congress, he could have avoided. Adam Clayton Powell could have passed for white and chose not to.

I was sorry we saw the inside of no other church. And when we drove

past a Muslim mosque, I'd have liked knowing whether it was the one from which Malcolm X first proclaimed to the people of Harlem that black was beautiful; but his name was never mentioned by the guide.

The tour made its final stop at a horribly dilapidated building on 135th Street which houses the Schomburg Collection, the largest collection of black history and art in the country, if not the world. But another Penny bus was parked in the only legal space available in front of it, so our tour bus had to bypass the collection. We learned later that we'd have seen very little of it even if we'd gone in. Most of the valuable art objects and manuscripts are packed away in crates, waiting for the new Schomburg museum building which was to have been built this year. The architect's plans were complete and the site selected, when the city's financial collapse put an end to the Schomburg's hopes of a decent home.

The bus rolled on down to 125th Street, Harlem's main shopping street (the guide told us that one of its two black-owned banks was founded by Johnny Mathis), and then on down through the terrible slums which were the only Harlem we'd ever read about: the burned and gutted buildings and uncleared piles of rubble that look like a bombed-out city, the inhabited tenements as desolate and unfit for human habitation as the abandoned buildings crumbling away beside them. It was a relief, at 116th Street, to turn east to Lexington Avenue, to the gaudy bedlam of the main shopping street of Spanish Harlem.

"It looks a little like Orchard Street," said Patsy as we peered out the window at the racks of dresses and cardboard packing cases overflowing with wigs and sweaters that filled the sidewalks. What was definitely not Orchard Street was the atmosphere: the Spanish signs above stores, the Latin music blaring from radios up and down the block and the staccato, stentorian Puerto Rican voices raised in the Puerto Rican English known as "Spanglish."

The bus turned down Fifth on its way back to Forty-second Street and the driver invited passengers to say where they'd like to be let off along the way. The two Australians wanted to get off at Seventy-ninth Street to visit the Natural History Museum, unaware that it was clear across the park on the West Side.

"They'll never find it," said Patsy. "I'm going to get off with them, I'll walk them across the park, I'd walk home that way anyway."

"Ask them how they found out about the tour," I said. All four of us got off at Seventy-ninth; Patsy and the Australians went west through the park, I walked down through it to Seventy-second and then home. On my way home, I bought a New York *Post*. I read the *Post* over lunch and then I phoned Patsy, knowing she'd have got home by then.

"What did you find out from the Australians?" I asked her.

"They're architecture students," she said enthusiastically. "They're over here on a six-month tour of the country; the Australian government's helping them. They've covered a thousand miles of this country in three months. They told me all about New Orleans and St. Louis!"

"What did you find out about the Harlem tour? How did they know about it?" I prodded.

"Oh," said Patsy. "I forgot to ask."

"Never mind," I said. "I have to call the tour guide anyway and give him the new celebrities in your building. Now then. Have you read the *Post*? Did you see what's opening to the public for the first time on May 29?"

"What?" asked Patsy.

"Ellis Island," I said.

"Oh, God," said Patsy. "My grandparents came to this country through Ellis Island. When can we go?"

"Monday?" I suggested.

"Monday's Memorial Day! We'll be away," said Patsy.

"Let's give it a week for the first crowds to thin out anyway," I said. "How's Friday, June 4? We'll get an early start and do the Stock Exchange, and stop at Trinity to check out that gravestone, and have lunch at Delmonico's and finish up at Ellis Island."

"It sounds like another blockbuster day," said Patsy.

"It should be," I said. "It's our last."

"Oh," said Patsy, sounding subdued, and we hung up.

The next morning I phoned the Penny Sightseeing Company and got the name and telephone number of our guide and phoned him. I gave him Patsy's new list of tenants ("Margaret Mead?" he said. "Oh my! Thank you very much.") and then I said:

"Will you tell me something? How did all the foreign tourists know about your tour?"

"Mrs. Penny has had fantastic publicity in European papers," he said. "Back in 1967, the A.P. ran a story on the tour and it was picked up by some European newspapers. And people over there who read about it took the tour when they came here, and then went home and wrote to their home-town newspaper: 'You were right, it's a great tour,' and that got her more publicity. And it just keeps mushrooming."

"Didn't the A.P. story run in American newspapers?" I asked.

"Oh yes," he said. "And the New York *Times* ran a story on us; the press has been very good to us."

"Then Americans do know about it," I said.

And he said, "Oh, yes."

I thanked him and hung up, still mystified. Two weeks later, when Patsy's son came home from college, he and a friend took the Penny tour, and they, too, were the only two Americans on a bus crowded with foreigners.

170

"I think I understand it," I said to Patsy when she relayed this information to me. "Foreigners are curious about our racial troubles, so a tour of Harlem attracts them. White Americans don't like thinking about our racial troubles, so they avoid the tour."

"And black Americans?" Patsy inquired. "They come to New York as tourists, too. Why don't they take the tour?"

Mystery unsolved.

38. MODEL SAILBOAT POND IN CENTRAL PARK
and the Model Boathouse, where I want you to press your nose
against the windows.

Saturday, May 29

From Memorial Day to Labor Day, New Yorkers divide into two groups: (1) those who always leave town on weekends, and (2) those who never leave town on weekends. Those of us in Group 2 have the standard negative reasons for staying home: we hate traveling on crowded highways and trains, and if we work all week and count on weekends to do our housekeeping chores, we hate coming home tired on a Sunday night to a dirty apartment, an overflowing laundry bag and an empty refrigerator.

But there's a positive reason that's equally potent. New York has a special charm for us on a summer weekend, when the town empties out, when the trucks and commuters and commuter cars are gone. The air is cleaner, the city is quieter, and the peaceful, empty avenues seem especially wide and beautiful. When we've had enough of the peace and quiet, we head for Central Park, where the action is.

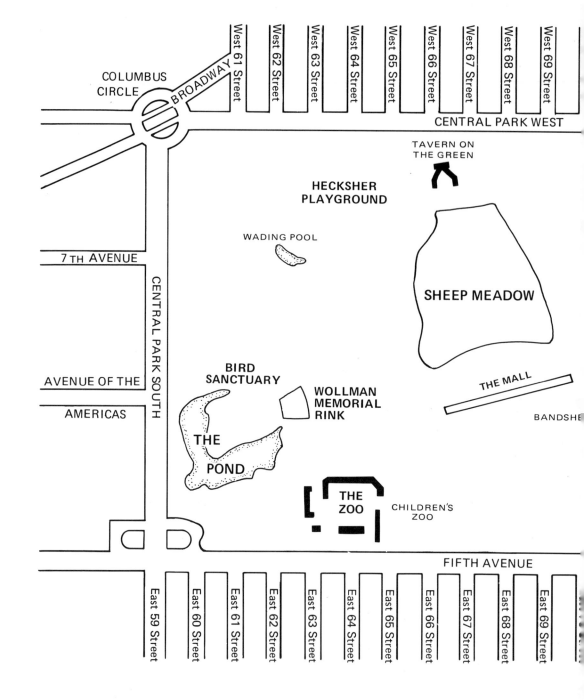

COLUMBUS
CIRCLE

BROADWAY

West 61 Street
West 62 Street
West 63 Street
West 64 Street
West 65 Street
West 66 Street
West 67 Street
West 68 Street
West 69 Street

CENTRAL PARK WEST

TAVERN ON
THE GREEN

HECKSHER
PLAYGROUND

WADING POOL

SHEEP MEADOW

7TH AVENUE

CENTRAL PARK SOUTH

BIRD
SANCTUARY

WOLLMAN
MEMORIAL
RINK

THE MALL

BANDSHE

AVENUE OF THE

AMERICAS

THE

POND

THE
ZOO

CHILDREN'S
ZOO

FIFTH AVENUE

East 59 Street
East 60 Street
East 61 Street
East 62 Street
East 63 Street
East 64 Street
East 65 Street
East 66 Street
East 67 Street
East 68 Street
East 69 Street

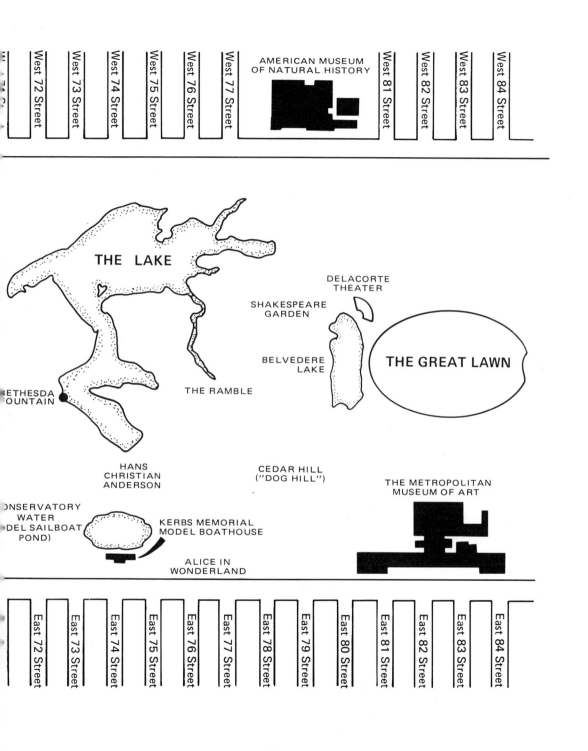

West 72 Street
West 73 Street
West 74 Street
West 75 Street
West 76 Street
West 77 Street
AMERICAN MUSEUM OF NATURAL HISTORY
West 81 Street
West 82 Street
West 83 Street
West 84 Street

THE LAKE

DELACORTE THEATER

SHAKESPEARE GARDEN

BELVEDERE LAKE

THE GREAT LAWN

THE RAMBLE

BETHESDA FOUNTAIN

HANS CHRISTIAN ANDERSON

CEDAR HILL ("DOG HILL")

THE METROPOLITAN MUSEUM OF ART

CONSERVATORY WATER (MODEL SAILBOAT POND)

KERBS MEMORIAL MODEL BOATHOUSE

ALICE IN WONDERLAND

East 72 Street
East 73 Street
East 74 Street
East 75 Street
East 76 Street
East 77 Street
East 78 Street
East 79 Street
East 80 Street
East 81 Street
East 82 Street
East 83 Street
East 84 Street

On weekdays the park itself is the town's only quiet, peaceful oasis. The playgrounds will be busy, and you'll pass a few baby-coach brigades, dog-walkers and teenage ball games; but there are vast, green empty stretches and I love it that way. On summer weekends the park is jammed and jumping and I love it that way.

So on Saturday of this first holiday weekend, I got up early to get my cleaning and marketing done by early afternoon and then headed for the park. Alone. On weekday afternoons, I go with my true love, a worried-looking, doe-eyed German shepherd named Duke, who lives on the sixteenth floor with parents who are at work all day and a brother who's in college. The park is more fun with a dog, and these days safer. I have never personally seen anyone or anything menacing in Central Park in all the years I've been going there, with or without a dog, you understand, but the newspapers' lurid accounts of muggings have made me cautious. If the newspapers printed—which they never do—equally lurid descriptions of car-crash victims, you'd learn to be cautious about your killer car. As it is, you probably know that cars kill and maim six hundred times as many people as muggers do, but you go on driving your car. I go on loving Central Park.

Today I went alone, partly because on a holiday weekend the park is too crowded for Duke. He's the longest German shepherd you ever saw, and if he chased a stick across a park lawn on a holiday weekend he'd wreck ten picnics. But mostly my mind was on this book, and on the secret of Central Park which only New Yorkers know about, and I went over there looking for signs of that secret.

There was the usual holiday jam at the Seventy-second Street entrance: crowds around the ice-cream and pretzel stands and a tangle of bikes and baby strollers, as cyclists and parents tried to work their way through the crowd and into the park. Just inside the entrance on my left, Nancy's playground was crowded with holiday fathers. Its bright red and yellow poles are faded and weatherbeaten now.

Nancy's playground (which doesn't have her name on it) is one of the small, preschool playgrounds you'll find at four- and five-block intervals throughout the park. One young mother used to call hers "The Snake Pit" because she was stuck in it all day every day, summer heat or winter snow, till her toddler graduated to one of the school-age playgrounds and could go without her. Well, about ten years ago, my friend Nancy was stuck in the Seventy-second Street playground with her two-year-old son. It was the usual antique playground with iron swings and a sandbox, and Nancy decided it ought to be modernized.

Nancy became chairwoman of a Mothers' Committee to raise funds for the project. She ran a big movie benefit and a fund-raising cocktail party, and finally the committee had enough money to hire a designer and finance the construction of new playground equipment. And one fine spring day the new playground opened, with bright red and yellow poles and a tree house and a turret house, and stone picnic benches and tables alongside the miniature wading pool.

But during the winter Nancy had gotten pregnant again, and she and Ed needed a larger apartment. By spring, when the new playground opened, they'd moved up to the Eighties over near the East River and Nancy was taking her two sons to Carl Schurz Park instead. And every time she rode downtown on a Fifth Avenue bus and saw the bright new playground from the bus window, she felt like Moses riding past the Promised Land.

On my right, across the road from Nancy's playground, a broad lawn slopes down to the Model Sailboat Pond with the Model Boathouse (a gift of the Kerbs family) alongside it. Press your nose against the boathouse door, and when your eyes have got used to the dark interior, you can see all the elaborate boats in dry dock: Columbus's fleet, pirate ships, whaling vessels, all fully rigged, and Spanish warships complete down to the galley slaves at the oars. The hobbyists who built them hold a regatta on a Sunday in June, and if you're here on the right Sunday it's something to see.

At the far end of the pond is the Alice in Wonderland Statuary, a gift of the Delacorte family, depicting the Mad Tea Party in bronze. A gigantic Alice presides over the tea table where the Dormouse, Cheshire Cat and March Hare are dominated by the Mad Hatter, or at least by the height of his mad hat. Older children climb to the top of Alice's head and sit on it, younger ones climb to the top of the Mad Hatter's hat, and toddlers crawl or stagger in and out among the giant mushrooms under the tea table.

(Alice in Wonderland is equaled in popularity only by the Children's Zoo down at Sixty-fifth in the park, the gift "To the Children of New York" of the late Governor and Mrs. Herbert Lehman. The Zoo buildings—including Noah's Ark and Old McDonald's Farm—are brightly colored and have entrance gates no higher than a five-year-old. You can see them from a Fifth Avenue bus window.)

On the western rim of the Sailboat Pond opposite the Model Boathouse, is Hans Christian Andersen. The great bronze figure sits at ease, leaning forward slightly, a book open on his left knee. His nose is worn shiny by the thousands of children's hands that have used it as a lever by which to hoist themselves up to sit piggyback around Hans Christian's neck.

But to see him properly, you have to visit Hans Christian with a child who has just learned to read, and who will climb up on Andersen's right knee and read aloud to you, from the open book on his left, the story of the Ugly Duckling. The duckling himself sits at Andersen's feet, listening with permanent bronze attention. This statue isn't as popular with children as Alice. But if you're a parent or grandparent, watching a child read from Andersen's book or a group of children sitting on the ground at his feet listening to the Story Lady from the New York Public Library read one of his fairy tales, you'll find the expression on Andersen's face very moving as he looks down at the children.

(At the back of the statue, an inscription in the stone explains that the statue was a gift to the children of New York from the children of Denmark.)

When Duke is with me, we walk north from the Sailboat Pond toward Dog Hill, and we usually pass the Clown on our way. Nobody seems to know who he is. All anybody knows is that on weekday afternoons he'll turn up in the park in a clown's motley and makeup, to sing and tell stories to the children who collect around him. I see him usually near Alice in Wonderland; friends of mine have seen him at other stations. Rumor has it he's a Wall Street stockbroker. But one Sunday when Duke and I were on our way to Dog Hill with our friends Richard and Chester-the-Sheepdog, we passed the Clown and I said:

"I've never seen him here before on a Sunday."

And Richard said:

"I thought he was taller. Are you sure this is the same Clown?"

The foot of Dog Hill is at Seventy-sixth Street and the hill slopes gradually upward to Seventy-ninth, rolling backward in a broad sweep as it rises. We claim it's the largest canine social hall in the world. On a sunny weekend afternoon, there'll be forty or fifty dogs charging around, two or three of whom always appoint themselves a welcoming committee and streak all the way down to the foot of the hill to greet every new arrival.

179

suburban commuters turn surly. (Their cars won't start and their trains run late.)
New Yorkers rush out and buy skis and sleds and head for Central Park, ecstatic.

It's the dream of my life to make enough money (which I won't) or leave enough money when I die (which I might) to donate a dog drinking-fountain to the Hill. If there's room on it for an inscription, it'll read:

To the dogs of New York City
From an Admirer

This town has got the friendliest, most sociable dogs you'll ever meet.

From Dog Hill, Duke and I usually push west to the Ramble, a small woods with winding paths and streams, and on over to the rowboat lake, where he goes swimming. Then we may walk up along the western bank and above it to see how Shakespeare's garden is coming along.

A month ago, the once-beautiful garden was a wasteland of dead flowerbeds and weeds, the decaying footbridge crumbling into the empty moat. The city has had no money for gardeners or workmen for several years. But during the past month, anonymous volunteers have been working in the garden, early every morning and on weekends. They've cleaned out the debris, and weeded and replanted and watered, and spread leaf cover over the worst-damaged plots, and the garden isn't what it was but it's beginning to grow again.

The garden is set on a high hill overlooking the Shakespeare theater, and Duke and I generally circle the theater coming back over to the East Side. Officially, it's the Delacorte Theater. But I suspect the Delacortes would agree that it ought to be called the Joe Papp theater instead.

Joe Papp began putting on free productions of Shakespeare in a clearing in the park back in 1954. Robert Moses was czar of the parks in those days and he demanded that Papp charge admission and use the money to pay the city for damage to the grass. Papp went to court to sue for the right to present Shakespeare free of charge. He won the suit. Moses asked the city to appropriate funds for a proper theater, to save the surrounding lawns, and the Delacortes—and thousands of anonymous New Yorkers—contributed the rest of the money. The theater opened in 1961 and seats three thousand people at free Shakespeare productions every summer, nightly-except-Monday.

Coming back east from the theater a couple of months ago, Duke and I passed a grove of newly planted pine trees at the far end of the lawn behind the Metropolitan Museum. The trees were planted by a man whose name I wish I remembered. I read about him in the *Times* a few days afterward. A *Times* reporter saw the man planting trees and asked him why he was doing it, and the man said he'd just happened to notice a bare stretch of ground at that end of the lawn and he thought a grove of evergreens would be nice.

Since Duke wasn't with me today, I didn't walk north from Seventy-second; I went a little south and west instead, to Central Park Mall. There's a bandshell at the entrance to it. The Naumberg Symphony Orchestra gives free concerts there on summer evenings—and also on holiday afternoons, which I didn't know till I got there today. There was an all-Mozart concert in progress when I went by, and the benches, which seat a thousand people, were almost completely filled. There are band concerts there, too. And I don't like band music but I'll have to go to the June 10 band concert, out of apartment-house loyalty. There's a Russian refugee couple in my building named Litkei. Mrs. Litkei is a retired ballerina; her husband is a musician. And this morning they put handbills under all the doors in our building (and all over the neighborhood on street-light poles and lobby tables) which read in part:

In the Name of All Foreign-Born Americans
in Grateful Appreciation to the United States of America
Erwin Litkei
proudly presents
The 26th U. S. Army Band . . .

How can you not go to that?

Beyond the bandshell, the Mall itself runs through the park for several blocks. Today's warm weather had brought out the food vendors—and I don't mean the usual pretzel, Italian-ice and hot-dog vendors. Along with the shish-kebab stands and Italian-sausage stands presided over by enterprising families, two young black men were broiling chicken and corn-on-the-cob over a charcoal fire, a middle-aged couple was cooking tacos and four young people sat behind a long table with two signs, one advising "SMILE! BE HAPPY!" and a smaller one advertising "Magic Foods to Turn You On!" The magic foods were apples, bananas, peaches, watermelon slices and coconuts. At one table, two girls were selling their homemade date-nut and pumpkin breads. Knowing they had potential customers in my building, I asked:

"Are you here every weekend?"

"I don't know," one of them answered uncertainly. "This is our first day."

Entertainers were performing to small crowds on the lawns beside the Mall. Two college students were doing rope tricks, a Puerto Rican band was playing Latin music and, at the far end, three students were playing a Haydn trio. A collection plate at their feet bore a sign explaining that classical music lessons cost money.

From the Mall I went west to the Sheep Meadow, where the Philharmonic and the Metropolitan Opera give performances on summer evenings, one Philharmonic concert drawing 250,000 people. The Sheep Meadow has an elastic seating capacity. There aren't any seats. You sit on the grass and keep inching over to make room for one more. (The concert and opera performances are paid for by private citizens and corporations, both usually anonymous.)

The size of the park—it's more than twice the size of Monaco—is a great boon on summer evenings. Down at the Wollman Skating Rink (gift of the Wollman family) the Schaefer Music Festival features rock-and-roll concerts (sponsored by the Schaefer Brewing Company). And loud as they are, the rock concerts are so far away that they never interfere with Mahler or Puccini holding forth on the Sheep Meadow—which in turn can't be heard by the actors or audience at the Shakespeare theater—which doesn't interfere with the sounds of the free Jazz Festival or Harlem Dance Theater performance going on up on the Harlem Mall.

Circling the Sheep Meadow and coming back east, I noticed the new green trash baskets. There are several hundred of them in the park now. The Central Park Community Task Force keeps adding batches of them with money raised by the Central Park Community Fund. Both organizations are composed of New Yorkers whose names wouldn't mean anything to you. They're trying to do for the park what the city can no longer afford to do. But there's a much older organization of volunteers called the

250,000 New Yorkers assembling on the Sheep Meadow in Central Park on a summer evening, for a free Philharmonic concert. (An hour later they were listening to Mahler in the darkness, with that skyline lit up above them.)

Friends of Central Park. Which brings us to Estelle, a fellow member of the Democratic club where Patsy and I first met and the guiding spirit behind the Friends of Central Park.

For years, Estelle has been the chief thorn-in-the-side of every city official, parks commissioner and private enterprise threatening her park. She has stood on picket lines outside the Metropolitan Museum of Art through one losing battle after another. And she fought harder than anyone else in the heartbreaking losing battle against the Metropolitan Transportation Authority, which is now engaged in ripping up whole acres of the park clear through from East Sixty-fourth to West Fifty-ninth to build a commuters' subway. Through Central Park. It's because of the yawning craters, and the old trees uprooted and destroyed to make room not only for a subway but for an MTA office building in the park, that I have described nothing in the park below Sixty-fifth Street. When you drive down Fifth Avenue, you'll see the ugly gray construction wall, the crude building and a glimpse of the havoc being wrought by the subway construction. And I can write "You'll see" with grim confidence—though I don't know when this book will be published or when you're coming to town. The office building, the wall, the subway construction and the ravaged park land will still be there. Count on it.

We thought Estelle would never recover from that blow, but she did. Fighting such juggernauts as the Metropolitan and the MTA, she loses

more battles than she wins, but she keeps bouncing back. She keeps on organizing picket lines and mass protests, raising money for a Tree Restoration Fund and demanding action from every new parks commissioner.

In recognition of which, there's to be a birthday party in Estelle's honor on July 21. More than a hundred of Estelle's friends have been invited to a Bring-Your-Own-Picnic Supper at the Central Park Lake boathouse, which is where Estelle wants it. Before the party, she'll receive an official Citation from the Mayor, to be presented to her by the Commissioner of Parks (if she's speaking to him). The party is in celebration of a milestone birthday of one of the most devoted of those unsung friends of Central Park who are the secret of its glory.

On July 21, Estelle will be ninety.

Since this was our last day, Patsy came over east and we took the Lexington Avenue IRT down to Wall Street together. We came up on the sidewalk in front of Trinity Church and I said:

"Let's get the inscription off that Tory's gravestone first. It'll only take a minute. The stone's at the edge of the cemetery; I read it from an outside path."

"I know," said Patsy. "It's on the Gallatin side." (The graveyard has two sections; Hamilton is buried in one, Gallatin in the other.)

We opened the gate and entered the churchyard, and stopped and stared with pleasure. The cemetery had been transformed by new plantings: flowering bushes where none had been before, even new trees where none had been before, and everywhere on the ground thick patches of green leaf cover.

"They've dressed it up for the Bicentennial!" I said.

We started along the outside path of the Gallatin side and Patsy, ahead of me, stopped at the spot where she remembered I'd read the inscription. There was no stone there. What *was* there was a large patch of green leaf cover backed by a flowering bush.

Some facts in this world you can accept. Now and then you're faced with a fact you can't accept.

"It must be further along," I said.

We moved along the outside path slowly, reading every stone. We circled the entire path. My Tory merchant wasn't there.

"He's on the Hamilton side," I said. And we went over to the Hamilton side and walked slowly along the outside path reading every stone. My Tory wasn't there.

We entered the cemetery grounds and picked our way among the inner paths, where we hadn't set foot before. We did every path, inch by inch, kneeling to read every stone, in a silence that got more and more pregnant. We did every path in both sections of the cemetery and it was a long time before we finally straightened and stared at each other.

"All these new bushes and leaves—" said Patsy tentatively.

"Exactly," I said. "They've covered that poor slob's stone with green leaves!"

"Let's go ask somebody," said Patsy.

We went into the church, but nobody was around at that early hour. There was, however, a rack of books and pamphlets inside the doorway, including a book labeled *History of Trinity Churchyard*. We carried it to a nearby bench and sat down to examine it.

Since we didn't know my Tory's name or birth-and-death dates, we couldn't find him. But reading a few pages, we did come upon mention of a deceased parishioner whose remains had been moved from the west section of the cemetery to the south, or maybe it was from the west to the north. And the book also contained a reminder that while Robert Fulton's opulent crypt was in Trinity churchyard, Robert Fulton wasn't.

We returned the book to its rack and left the church and walked through the churchyard in silence. But as we passed the spot where we were certain the plaque-or-stone had been, Patsy stopped. She stared down at the leaves and the flowering bush, and shook her head in disbelief.

"It's remarkable," she said in an awed tone. "In this town, you not only get pushed around all your life, you get pushed around after you're dead!"

"I'm getting to the bottom of this," I said. "Tomorrow morning, I'm phoning Trinity Church."

(The next morning I looked up Trinity Church in the Manhattan phone book. I stared at the listing for several minutes. Then I pulled myself together and phoned Patsy. "Go look up Trinity Church in the phone book," I said. "I'll wait." And we gawked at it together for five minutes before we hung up.

(I defy you to find another city in which a church parish takes up half a column in the phone book, with a total of forty-seven separate phone numbers. Forty-six are for the Rector, Associate Rector, Deputy Outreach & Planning, Parish Administration, Parish Resources, Parochial Ministries, also Accounting, Administration, Budget, Buildings, Camp & Conferences, Cemetery Ofc., Chapels, Clerk, Communications, Food, Maintenance, Personnel, Purchasing, Real Estate and Schools. The forty-seventh is for All Other Business, of which it's a little hard to think of any. Not wanting to be transferred from Cemetery Ofc. to Administration to Outreach, I abandoned the phone and wrote a letter to the rector, asking politely whether my Tory had been moved elsewhere or just covered with leaves.

(I received a charming reply but not until the rector had worn himself out trying to locate my merchant's name and stone-or-plaque for me.

Without success. Letters flew back and forth between us, and finally he wrote to say that while Trinity had, in former times, moved gravestones from section to section when it wasn't sure where they rightly belonged, this practice had been discontinued a generation ago, and my Tory was therefore probably under the leaves. The rector himself hoped to search for the gentleman on the first winter day when the leaves were gone.)

We left Trinity, and Patsy headed across the street to check the side wall of the Irving Trust. There was no new plaque, only the pale square of stone where the old one had been. Patsy went into the bank to inquire, innocently, about the missing plaque. I reached her side just as a bank official was saying regretfully:

"Vandals stole it, I'm afraid."

"It was only a plaque, it had no historical value," I said as if I'd never said it before. "Couldn't the bank afford to have a new one made?"

And he said, with as much huffy reproof as if *he'd* never said it before:

"I'm sure the bank is doing that."

As we left the bank Patsy, glancing from the blank spot on the wall to Trinity churchyard across the street, said morosely:

"One thing about the Stock Exchange: it'll *be* there."

The Wall Street entrance to the New York Stock Exchange is for members and employees only. Tourists go around the corner to 20 Broad Street and up to the third or "Visitors'" floor.

We stepped out of the elevator and a receptionist waved us toward the Visitors' Gallery, a long hall to the right of the reception desk. A plate-glass window runs the length of the hall and we went up to the window and found ourselves looking directly down onto the Floor of the Exchange two floors below. Other visitors were lined up alongside us and a guide was explaining the functions of everything we saw below us: the "Big Board" with its listing of stocks traded, the electronic ticker which has replaced

44. "ULCER ALLEY"
Note that the entire Stock Exchange Floor was built below ground,
like a dungeon.

ticker tape, the trading stations and the men and women whose blue, maroon or gray jackets identified them as brokers or assistants or runners. A few customers stood behind the entranceway to the Exchange, their eyes on the electronic ticker panel.

"You know what brokers call this?" a man standing next to me said to his companion, pointing down to the Floor. "Ulcer Alley."

From the gallery, the guide led us down the opposite hall, and after seeing a few exhibits there, we filed into a small theater to see a cartoon film entitled: "One-Man Band Goes to Wall Street." The cartoon story of how a small company grows large enough to be listed on the Big Board was entertaining; but its high-school-textbook explanation won't give you any practical grasp of how the stock market works. The difference between the film's theory and Ulcer Alley's practice was underscored by the contrast between the gay insouciance of the cartoon and the grim, unsmiling faces on the Exchange Floor. As I remarked to Patsy when we left:

"It's a nice place to visit but I wouldn't want to live there."

The Delmonico restaurant (not to be confused with the restaurant in the Hotel Delmonico on Park Avenue) is at the corner of Beaver and South William streets. We were going there for our final celebration lunch because an article in *New York* magazine suggested it might be a tourist attraction. It is.

One of Patsy's clippings said that the original Delmonico's had gone bankrupt and closed in 1917. But walking into the present restaurant, we found that hard to believe. Where Fraunces Tavern has been "restored" with self-conscious charm, Delmonico's seems never to have changed at all; it looks exactly as it must have looked a hundred years ago. To walk through the vestibule into the grandiose saloon with its heavy mahogany bar, and then push through the swinging doors into the restaurant, is to walk back into the 1870s. From the patterned brocade wallpaper and heavy iron sconces to the ornate chandeliers with their load of small green lampshades, everything seems to be just as it always was. If you remember *Life with Father*, you'll find yourself glancing at the door, half-expecting to see Father Day shepherding the family and Cousin Cora in to his accustomed table.

My friend Richard has a cookbook entitled *The Epicurean*, compiled by the Delmonico chef and published in 1920, which I covet and can't get him to part with. The cookbook requires 1,180 pages to hold the laborious recipes and gargantuan menus which made Delmonico famous in the gluttonous Edwardian days when it was the scene of ten-course testimonial dinners to President Grant, the Grand Duke Alexis of Russia, Charles Dickens and Ferdinand de Lesseps.

The modern menu has shrunk to fit modern stomachs, though the food is still good (and still expensive). But it's less the food than the evocation of a bygone era that makes lunch at Delmonico's worth the price.

When we came out, we could see Battery Park a few blocks below us, and we walked down to the park ticket booth where, on our first sightseeing day, we had bought tickets for the ferry to the Statue of Liberty.

"We've come full circle," said Patsy.

The Ellis Island ticket booth was next to the Liberty Island booth and we bought tickets and waited with other tourists to board the ferry. A

guide rode to the island on the ferry with us and warned us, on the way, that twenty-odd years of disuse had left the island's buildings badly eroded by water and weather. The wooden beams above the main hall, he said, had so rotted away that fences had to be thrown up to prevent injury to tourists from falling beams, before the island could be opened to the public. (The National Park Service, which oversees Ellis Island, has had its budget severely cut by Congress.)

As the ferry drew alongside the dock, we saw the hulk of the original ferry, the *Ellis Island*, still at anchor. The *Ellis Island* had met the immigrants as their ships docked in New York harbor, and ferried them to Ellis Island for medical and legal processing before they were allowed to set foot in the New World. Those who failed the medical and legal examinations never would set foot in it.

We were taken to the Main Hall, a vast room where the immigrants were separated into national groups, and tagged, before they were sent on to the examination rooms. Opening off the room we saw ancient lavatories —and heard an elderly man behind us say:

"That's it! That's where we washed!"

We saw the dormitory rooms where the immigrants slept, and the medical examination rooms where those found to have tuberculosis or trachoma, or any other incurable or contagious disease, were denied entry. When the breadwinner of a family had bad lungs or a faulty heart, the whole family might be rejected, since they might become public charges without him. More terrible still was the plight of a healthy family in which a single child was found to have TB. The family had to decide whether to give up its chance at a new life in America and return to Europe, or send the child back to the Old World alone. The legal examination consisted of questions: "Can you read and write? Have you a job here? Who offered you the job? Who paid for your passage?"

198

These last two questions were designed to weed out the "undesirables": prostitutes, spies, revolutionaries and strike-breakers. Strike-breakers were the most numerous. The island's peak years were 1892 to 1929, when Labor was organizing its first major strikes for decent wages and working conditions. The great steel companies and railroads went to lengths to import cheap immigrant labor with which to break the strike. (See the Frick Collection, Carnegie Hall, Rockefeller University . . .)

Rejected immigrants were isolated in a special building on the island to await the ships that had brought them to America and were now required to pick them up and return them to Europe. But most of the immigrants had nothing to go back to. They'd sold everything—house, land, farm tools, possessions—to raise passage-money for the trip. There's a water tower above the main building on Ellis Island. And during the night, when no guards were on watch, rejected immigrants climbed to the top of the tower and jumped to their deaths. Five thousand bodies of immigrants were burned in mass cremations on the island, since there was no money for burial. How many more immigrants were drowned and their bodies never recovered, nobody will ever know.

Such stories were bearable to us because we were told that the overwhelming majority of immigrants—98 per cent of them—were accepted. After days of harrowing uncertainty, they were given legal and medical clearance, were put aboard the *Ellis Island* once more, were ferried past the Statue of Liberty into New York harbor, where they stepped ashore, home free.

As we were leaving, I looked back at the great, empty Main Hall, more dilapidated but probably no more grim and forbidding now than when the immigrants were herded into it, tense and frightened, to await the all-important examinations. Standing there with Patsy Gibbs at my side—granddaughter of Ellis Island immigrants, whose children will be second-generation Harvard graduates—it seemed to me that every New York sight we had seen, from one end of the island to the other, was insignificant compared with the gaunt and crumbling wreck of Ellis Island.

It was after five when we finally stepped ashore at Battery Park and walked once more, as we had on our first day, up to the broad intersection leading into the city. As we waited for a green light, the canyons and towers of Lower Manhattan stretched ahead of us; and every street and skyline grouping was familiar.

"We own this city now," said Patsy. "Do you feel that way?"

"I've been defensive about it for so long," I said. "Every TV newsman tells me the city is dying, every newspaper story harps on crime and bankruptcy—and then you see a headline reading 'FORD TO NEW YORK: DROP DEAD.' It gets to you, without your realizing it. I'll never be defensive about it again. It's a marvelous city."

Patsy was standing rooted to the sidewalk, her mouth open, her eyes wide with shock.

"Defensive!" she repeated in a scandalized voice. "Are you crazy? This is the most fabulous city on earth!"

And we walked on peacefully through the narrow streets toward the subway we could take together as far as Grand Central.

"I don't see how this can be our last trip," said Patsy. "There have to be places we didn't see!"

"A few," I said. "Four hundred art galleries. Forty museums. Two hundred-and-something landmark houses. SoHo. Astor Place. We never took the helicopter trip from Thirty-fourth Street up over Central Park. But I've got a deadline on this book, and all I've written so far is a thick book of notes and a Prologue."

We went down the subway steps and put our tokens in the turnstile. The platform was crowded—it was the five o'clock rush hour—and we stood off to one side by ourselves. I looked at Patsy's face and wondered if mine looked the same.

"You know," I said, "we can come down here again. It's probably slipped your mind, but we live here! We can do the whole tour over again, any time we want to!"

But we knew we never would. We'd been on a holiday and the holiday was over. I was on my way back to my typewriter; Patsy was on her way back to her family. In a few days, we'd have settled back into the routines of our separate lives.

The subway train roared into the station, splitting eardrums as usual. As it screeched to a halt, Patsy turned to me and shouted:

"It was the best two months I ever had!"

"Me, too!" I shouted back.

The doors opened and we squeezed into a car jammed to the doors with rush-hour riders. But the densely packed bodies somehow shifted, willing, as always, to make room for two more tired New Yorkers on their way home.

46. DYING CITY

HELENE HANFF was born in Philadelphia but has lived for many years in New York. She has written many books, most notable 84, CHARING CROSS ROAD, and its sequel THE DUCHESS OF BLOOMSBURY.